CROWOOD COLLECTORS' SERIES

Action Figures

FROM ACTION MAN TO ZELDA

CROWOOD COLLECTORS' SERIES

Action Figures

FROM ACTION MAN TO ZELDA

ARTHUR WARD

THE CROWOOD PRESS

First published in 2020 by
The Crowood Press Ltd
Ramsbury, Marlborough
Wiltshire SN8 2HR

enquiries@crowood.com

www.crowood.com

British Library Cataloguing-in-Publication Data
A catalogue record for this book is available from the British Library.

ISBN 978 1 78500 687 6

Frontispiece
Large and small GI Joe – full-size Hasbro GI Joe and 1:35 scale Takara GI Joe's GI Joe.

Contents
Kenner 'Small Soldiers' (1998) 'Gorgonite Archer' and 'Chip Hazard' of the Commando Élite.

Typeset by Jean Cussons Typesetting, Diss, Norfolk
Printed and bound in India by Parksons Graphics

DEDICATION

For my mother and father, who initiated my lifelong passion for action figures by buying my first GI Joe when we lived in Hong Kong, more than half a century ago.

And for my daughters, Eleanor and Alice, who have long been obliged to tolerate their father's fascination for old toys.

ACKNOWLEDGEMENTS

Although responsibility for the words and photographs is entirely mine, I was lucky enough to benefit from the help and advice of several people who each significantly contributed to the value of this book. My sincere thanks, in alphabetical order, to Carol and Peter Allen, Lisa Bessinger, Bob Brechin, Ralph Ehrmann, Dave Grey, Mark Grundy, Keith Melville, Nick Millen and Jade Nodinot.

Other than the occasional copy of an advertisement or product leaflet, the great majority of the photography in this book is my own. However, four photographs are the copyright of Mark Grundy: the 'Action Man Jeep and Trailer', the 'Action Man Tank Commander', the 'Action Man French Resistance Fighter', and the 'Action Man Green Beret' outfit. Thanks Mark.

My good friend Dave Grey is responsible for the cool Photoshop work on the Action Man 7th Cavalry figure.

However, the frontispiece image I took featuring GI Joe holding a smaller figure is not the result of such Photoshop manipulation: the 12-inch figure is holding a 1:35-scale miniature action figure that was produced by Takara in 2004.

Trademarks and Brand Ownership

'GI Joe', 'Action Man', 'Action Soldier', 'Action Marine', 'Action Pilot', 'Action Sailor' and 'America's Moveable Fighting Man' are all © & ™ Hasbro Inc.

Star Wars, The Force, The Dark Side & Star Wars action figures © & ™ Lucas Films Ltd, The Walt Disney Company, Hasbro Inc.

Airfix is a registered trademark © Hornby Hobbies Ltd.

Iron Man © &™ Marvel Entertainment, LLC, a wholly owned subsidiary of The Walt Disney Company.

Superman, Batman, Batwoman, Batgirl, Catwoman © &™DC Comics, Inc. the publishing unit of DC Entertainment, a subsidiary of Warner Bros.

Barbie, Ken, Skipper, Hot Wheels, Fisher Price, American Girl, Mega Bloks and Jurassic World are all © &™Mattel Inc.

Ballad of the Green Berets © Staff Sgt. Barry Sadler.

Mego is a trademark of Marty Abrams Presents Mego.

INTRODUCTION

Something very unusual happened to American youth during the 1964 Christmas vacation. As children explored the bounty of presents lying beneath festive trees, one gift elicited such a reaction of rapture from the boys amongst them that it flew in the face of established behaviour. Amongst anticipated gender-specific gifts such as Louis Marx's 'Rock 'Em, Sock 'Em' robots, Aurora's 'Nuclear Airliner' model kit or J.C. Higgins' shiny and streamlined battery-powered 'Rocket Jet' bike headlight, the one they unwrapped most feverishly was... a doll.

Well, not a doll *precisely*. For although it was of similar height to Barbie, whose hour-glass physique had graced little girls' bedrooms since 1959, and also came complete with a range of outfits and accessories to rival that fashionista's wardrobe, GI Joe, for that is what this 'doll' was, differed from Barbie in a couple of very important ways. Firstly, he was what was called an 'action figure', never a doll. And secondly, guns rather than clutch bags were his accoutrements of choice.

Retailing at just $4 apiece, GI Joe was also a most affordable toy; in its inaugural year manufacturer Hasbro sold $23 million worth of figures and accessories, a remarkable sum for the time. When America's 'Movable Fighting Man' crossed the pond in 1966 to be licence-built in Leicestershire by Hasbro licensee Palitoy, he was an equal success, and after a name change to Action Man, was voted Toy of the Year on his British debut. In fact, most enthusiasts agree that Palitoy were responsible for making much more of the toy line than Hasbro ever did during its eighteen-year tenure. For their part, Palitoy had settled on a product that sold far better than anything else they had ever manufactured, achieving the remarkable production statistic of an astounding thirty million of the 12-inch giants.

The summer following GI Joe's introduction, Rosko Industries, one of Hasbro's many competitors, succeeded in persuading Sears, then the retailer with the largest domestic revenue in the United States, to stock their 'Johnny Hero' figure, which marked the first of countless significant copies of GI Joe. However, even though, just like Hasbro's toy, 'Johnny Hero' came dressed in combat gear and carried a rifle,

Action Man 7th cavalry figure.

can boys occurred is the stuff of legend and the subject of this book: their new-found enthusiasm has spread rapidly around the globe and so completely that today, action figures are now amongst the most popular toys in the world.

Hornby Gladiators' 'Wolf' action figure (1992).

Product Enterprises' white 'Talking Dalek' (2001). On its launch, Stephen Walker, the company's founder, said 'The radio-controlled Dalek has been the star of the toy fairs this spring'.

because the term 'action figure' had not yet entered common parlance, Rosko's product was classified as a 'boy's doll', which naturally didn't do the toy's prospects any favours.

The phenomenal success of GI Joe revealed that, just like their sisters, boys would happily play with miniature articulated figures, and got just as much pleasure from dressing them up in different ensembles before they imbued them with a life and, through them, let their imagination soar.

Just how this sea-change in the tastes of Ameri-

PLASTIC TOYS COME OF AGE

Children have played with toys for millennia. Archaeological excavations of Bronze Age settlements in the Indus Valley have revealed toy whistles that are still capable of holding a tune, and have even exposed concatenated miniature animals featuring movable limbs and jaws – action figures, of sorts, from prehistory. Egyptian children amused themselves with wooden or pottery toy dolls complete with articulated limbs, and which even featured miniature wigs composed of braided hair. Roman youngsters were entertained by pushing along wheeled terracotta horses – they even had toy yo-yos.

When Greek children, especially girls, reached maturity, they were encouraged to put away such childish things, sacrificing them to the gods instead. In most cultures however, such extravagant destruction was avoided, for whether simple or complex, toys required a lot of effort to produce and as such were precious items to be cherished.

For centuries toys remained bespoke items, individual pieces fashioned by hand, often whittled from a piece of wood or assembled from scraps of woven fabric and stuffed with horsehair or goose down. To ensure their durability, toys took time to construct and were of such quality that they endured to be coveted by successive generations of children – treasured hand-me-downs made to last.

Toys for the Many

The industrial revolution changed all this. The rapid production of identical components and the result-

ant series assembly of commercial products enabled mass production, providing quality manufactured goods for the many and not just the privileged few. At last, an assortment of fabricated items – including toys – could be produced economically. For the first time, by the eighteenth century inexpensive toys were available for sale in shops, bedecking shelves alongside long-familiar utilitarian items.

And there was more: the revolution in paper manufacture, allied with the step-change developments that had revolutionized printing technology, now enabled the production of cheaper, less robust games and novelties such as pop-up books and toy theatres. Before long, what we now know as board games were also being enjoyed, and with the release of 'Journey through Europe' in 1759, John Jefferys produced the first. In 1761 came another major development, when cartographer John Spilsbury created the first jigsaw puzzle.

However, despite the appearance of such revolutionary egalitarianism, some toys remained out of reach of the masses until well into the nineteenth century. This was principally because a large proportion of them were still made from relatively expensive materials, such as heavy cast metal – and because lighter tinplate products generally featured hand-painted or litho-printed decoration, even these substantially flimsier objects remained costly. Thus for a long time, playthings were but a dream for the children of working-class families. Anyway, such progeny had no time for toys: they often spent their daylight hours toiling in factories and mills, and rarely had the opportunity to enjoy the luxury of playtime.

However, the advent of inexpensive lead diecasting at the turn of the twentieth century levelled the playing field as far as the production of cheap and easy novelties and knick-knacks was concerned. Although the hand-painted figures produced by William Britain weren't cheap, many other toy soldiers could be purchased for pennies. Zinc alloys such as Mazak also meant that toy vehicles were now within reach of even the most restricted pocket. The 'toffs' could keep their delicate tinplate and parade-ground assemblies of artisan-finished soldiers, while ordinary children relished playing with diecast vehicles and roughly painted lead soldiers that stood up to any amount of rowdiness.

The new century even saw legislation restrict the use of child labour, which at last granted them some free time. Although it still promised oppressive prospects for those unfortunates aged thirteen or over, a 1901 Act forbade children under the age of twelve from working. Until then, incredibly, the law had permitted children aged nine or over to work up to sixty hours per week, night or day.

The Arrival of Plastic

However, it wasn't until the arrival of plastic that the combination of truly inexpensive 'pocket-money' toys, and the freedom to enjoy them, transformed children's playtime. Certainly without plastics, action figures, the subject of this book, would have remained out of reach to the many, just as in Victorian times dolls with porcelain bisque heads were only accessible to the privileged few. As far as action figures are concerned, plastic was the game-changer.

Plastic is a man-made material formed from mouldable polymers of a high molecular mass capable of deforming irreversibly without breaking; polymers also exist in nature in the form of shellac, amber, wool, silk and natural rubber. Polymers are even present in DNA and proteins. We are more familiar with plastic in its synthetic form, especially in its most common manifestations: polyethylene, polypropylene, polystyrene and polyvinyl chloride, the latter two materials being the basis of most of the figures in this book.

One of the British names most closely associated with plastic, Airfix started life in 1939, manufacturing inflatables, novelties and cheap plastic toys, such as these soldiers, which date from 1948.

For a short while, however, prior to the advent of polystyrene and PVC, another, now less well-known plastic, enjoyed its moment in the sun. Briefly cellulose, the main constituent of wood and paper, reigned supreme. An important structural component of the primary cell walls of green plants, cellulose is the most abundant organic polymer on Earth. The cellulose content of cotton fibre, for example, is 90 per cent, while that of wood is 40–50 per cent. Today, cellulose is mainly used to produce paperboard and paper, but after its discovery in 1838 by the French chemist Anselme Payen, it served as the basis for the first successful thermoplastic polymer, celluloid.

Celluloid

Patented in 1869 by American John Wesley Hyatt, celluloid was initially used to make billiard balls and spectacle frames. A decade later, he was granted the patent for injection moulding the material, and the resulting possibilities were endless. In 1887 the Rev Hannibal Goodwin patented celluloid film, which became a staple of the photographic and movie industry for many years to come. By the turn of the century, celluloid was the main constituent in the manufacture of combs, causing a terminal decline in the popularity of tortoiseshell and horn, both previously the principal components in the manufacture of such items.

Prior to the introduction of celluloid, dolls were extremely fragile, with bodies of china or papier-mâché, heads of bisque, and limbs that were often formed from wax. They were collectable items more suitable for display, rather than for the antics of the nursery. England, Bavaria, France, Japan, Poland and the USA were the principal manufacturers of the new, cheaper, and more robust celluloid dolls. Despite the material being further improved in 1908, celluloid nitrate, to give the material its full name, was certainly not the answer to everything. Difficult to work, it was also unstable, and because it was an explosive polymer, it had the unfortunate habit of being readily flammable. Readers of a certain age might recall that even after 35mm acetate film replaced celluloid in the 1950s, for decades afterwards, the frame edges remained marked with the legend 'safety film'.

Set of 'Beatlemania' figures by Spanish firm Emirober (1964).

Before he joined Airfix and ultimately Hasbro, owners of GI Joe, Peter Allen did a five-year engineering draughtsman's apprenticeship at Lines Bros, owners of Tri-ang and the Arkitex plastic 'Girder-and-panel' construction set shown here, with which, for a short time, he found himself involved. Peter worked with the product's designer, Geoff Bailey, whom he remembers as a 'great guy, a fantastic boss who was always very encouraging'. Peter's job utilized all his model-making skills as he prepared prototype models for the Toy Fair.

Despite its imperfections, the introduction of celluloid encouraged a frenzy of invention, and was the catalyst for a thermoplastics gold rush.

Bakelite

In 1899 Arthur Smith patented phenol-formaldehyde resins to replace ebonite for electrical insulation. Five years later, in 1904, Sir James Swinburne, the 'Father of British Plastics', formed The Fireproof Celluloid Syndicate and later, joined forces with Belgian Chemist Leo Baekeland to establish the Damard Lacquer Company, which in turn evolved into Bakelite, the famous brand name for the first truly successful thermoset phenol-formaldehyde material. Bakelite immediately assumed a position previously enjoyed by natural materials such as wood, ivory and ebonite, and very soon a wide range of everyday items were henceforth made synthetically. Unlike nitrate cellulose, Bakelite proved a truly stable and durable plastic, capable of being moulded into an infinite variety of household goods from radio cabinets to picture frames, bookshelves and lamp cases. Furthermore Bakelite was not a potential fire hazard. Because of its superb properties for electrical insulation, Bakelite is still in use today, especially in the automotive industry where it is employed under the hood of motor vehicles in a myriad hidden applications.

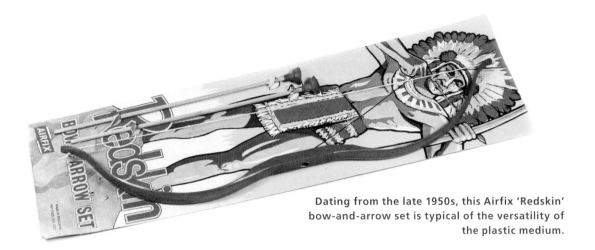

Dating from the late 1950s, this Airfix 'Redskin' bow-and-arrow set is typical of the versatility of the plastic medium.

Formica, another material that was initially developed as an electrical insulator, first appeared in 1910. This most utilitarian product was followed by an ultimately even more significant one, when in 1912, Russian Ivan Ostromislensky patented the polymerization of vinyl chloride, and PVC was born, a material that is also still very much part of our world today.

Polystyrene

Baekeland had patented the specific heat and pressure processes essential to forming his plastic mate-

rial into its final form, but these patents expired in 1927. The year before, Germans Eckert and Ziegler had produced the first commercially successful injection-moulding machine, and this proved most suitable for moulding the rival plastics that now competed with Bakelite – especially polystyrene, a material synthesized by another German, Eduard Simon, back in 1839. The Germans were clearly the leaders in synthetics and chemical production, and in 1927 another Teuton, Otto Rohm, developed methyl methacrylate – the first clear plastic.

In 1937 Hans Kellerer, an Austrian this time, further perfected the injection-moulding process, introduc-

US toy firm Louis Marx's answer to Hasbro's ground-breaking GI Joe action figure was 'Stony (Stonehouse) Smith'. As this photograph shows, Marx took full advantage of the potential of plastic moulding, arming their soldier to the teeth with copious accessories.

ing a fully automatic machine capable of continuous operation.

Another significant leap forwards occurred in 1930 when America's DuPont corporation began researching the properties of nylon, and in 1935 they produced the first commercially viable synthetic fibre.

It wasn't until BASF and Dow Chemical had completed their development work earlier in the 1930s that polystyrene, the other significant modern plastic, came to prominence. By 1937 the full-scale production of injection-moulded polystyrene had consigned cellulose to the trash can of history, well for everything other than, for a short period, photographic film. In company with this breakthrough, by 1939 chemists at ICI added the discovery of low-density polyethylene (LDPE) to the inventory of modern plastics. Their work resulted in a revolution in the manufacture of robust household products such as bowls and bottles, and, to society's contemporary cost, the production of plastic bags.

In 1940, the USA was the first country to completely outlaw the use of volatile celluloid in toys. Having more serious matters to attend to perhaps, Britain and Germany didn't follow suit until 1945. And anyway, during the war, Britain's largest toymaker, Lines Bros (Tri-ang), were obliged to switch from the production of children's scooters to the manufacture of Sten guns in support of the war effort.

Postwar Development of Synthetic Products

With the coming of peace, toymakers quickly embraced the range of new polymers now available. Previously these had been the sole province of the military industrial complexes of rival belligerents and used for the manufacture of the myriad switches, dials, stocks, pistol grips, oxygen masks and instrument binnacles employed in weapon systems.

By this time, however, polystyrene, polyvinyl chloride (PVC) and polyethylene were available to use for more peaceful pursuits. Capable of being fashioned at high speed in the new moulding machines avail-

able for commercial exploitation, there appeared to be no limit to the available possibilities.

Japan's wartime conquests in Asia and their consequent stranglehold on rubber production was another critical factor in the development of synthetic products, encouraging the allies' urgent search for synthetic alternatives to latex. The war also obliged another of the original protagonists, Nazi Germany, to explore synthetics. The dramatic reversal of their fortunes soon after the invasion of Russia and the Caucasus saw the loss of the precious oil supplies previously taken for granted. Remarkably, before the Third Reich collapsed in 1945, Hitler's Germany had become largely self-sufficient, its chemists notching up breakthrough after breakthrough.

Imperceptibly, by osmosis almost, the steady transition from very physical manual labour, often in an outdoor, agrarian setting, towards fixed hours in a factory or office, was all but complete by the dawn of the twentieth century. Peoples' lives were transformed forever. One positive benefit of all this was that workers now enjoyed regulated leisure time. Successive laws also restricted the employment of child labour, and most youngsters now stayed at home after attending school or perhaps participated in less onerous work, such as part-time jobs like paper rounds or assisting the milkman with his deliveries.

Initially known as adolescents, by the 1950s a new social group, now called teenagers, had come to the fore. A by-product of American rock-and-roll, this new constituency was something new: a large, reasonably affluent group with time and spending money on their hands. Advertisers and brand owners loved them.

Increased prosperity also meant that even if such youngsters didn't have jobs, many of them received regular pocket money or allowances, and it wasn't long before the commercial world found ways of relieving them of this bounty. 45rpm records quickly became the almost exclusive province of older teenagers, but younger ones still played with, or collected toys, and at last all the technological and sociological advances converged to make them cheaply and readily available.

CHINA IN THE ASCENDANT

Action figures are an American creation, and GI Joe was the first. The British improved the concept, and most enthusiasts agree that Action Man is his smarter cousin, equipped with better uniforms and accessories and enjoying special features such as flocked hair and gripping hands, which meant that for the first time these fighting men could hold their guns properly!

Other European manufacturers such as Pedigree and Madelman further developed the genre. However, it was Hong Kong-based companies that elevated the design and consequently the appeal of action figures to even higher levels. Ironically, the originally GI Joe doll featured a scar that was cunningly intended to be a tell-tale, revealing if Chinese manufacturers had simply taken an impression from one of Hasbro's toys and used it to cast a mould from which an infinite number of copies could be issued. By the late 1990s Chinese toy companies weren't simply intending to follow – they led the way, the efforts of Hasbro, Palitoy and the like being left far behind, as historic anachronisms.

One of the first Hong Kong-based toy companies to enter the action-figure market wasn't a newcomer at all, but one that had been around for quite a while. Blue Box Toys (BBI) was founded in 1952 by the late Peter Chan Pui, a man who spent sixty years working in the toy industry, and who in 2011 was presented with the Outstanding Achievement Award by the Hong Kong Toys Council. The first Blue Box toy, the famous 'Drinks and Wets' doll, was the first of a successful range of toys that saw the company establish factories in both Hong Kong and Singapore, and in the 1980s, on mainland China. With a broad range of infant and pre-school toys for girls and boys at its core, Blue Box has also developed electronic toys and other collectable items.

In 2000 Blue Box entered the action-figure market with a range of figures based on popular video games, such as Omega Boost and Fighting Force. In 2001 they produced 'Élite Force', a range of 12-inch military Special Forces figures, notable because of their revolutionary custom expression mechanism, by which facial expressions could be adjusted by turning a small screw in the back of the head, continuous product R&D being at the heart of Blue Box's manufacturing ethos.

Blue Box Toys' collectables arm, bbicollectable.com, home to the finest miniatures, markets Élite Force figures and vehicles in three scales: 1:6, 1:18 and 1:32. Boxed 1:6-scale figures, such as 'Sgt Bones Wilson', a US Air Force para-rescue soldier, and a strikingly garbed 'US Navy Desert Ops Seal Team' member equipped for HAHO (High Altitude High Opening) operations, are especially notable.

In 2014 Blue Box became partners with established American retailer Target to make a new, non-military series of 1:6 scale 'Wild Adventure' action figures available. Themed as both non-military and non-super heroic, and focusing instead on classic all-American sporting pursuits such as hunting and fishing, these new figures were only available online from Target's website.

Established in 1987, Hong Kong-based Dragon Models Limited (Dragon, or DML) introduced its first 1:6 scale 'New Generation' action figure series in 1999, and since then has become one of the premier manufacturers of 'traditional' action figures in the world. (As such they are entitled to their own specific box, where much more information about this exciting company, a leader in action figures and, especially, in high-quality construction kits, can be found.)

In 1997 21st Century Toys began producing 1:6-scale accessory and uniform sets representing equipment used in the Vietnam War, and soon expanded their product line to include World War II, law enforcement, the emergency services, and modern armed forces' accessories under the brand names 'The Ultimate Soldier' (TUS) and 'America's Finest' respectively. The company offered more detail and historical accuracy than Hasbro had previously managed. 21st Century further expanded their line to include vehicles and a 'Villains' series. In 1999, the company further improved their designs with the introduction of the 'Super Soldier' body design, which featured no fewer than twenty-seven movable parts.

(continued overleaf)

CHINA IN THE ASCENDANT *(continued)*

Blue Box (BBI) 'Elite Force Pearl Harbor pilot' box outer (2002).

For some reason World War II German designs have always proved the most popular with consumers – just ask plastic construction kit manufacturers such as Italeri and Tamiya – and it was the same for action figures. 21st Century Toys regularly received complaints about the preponderance of Nazi soldiers from the Third Reich in their range, whilst their competitors, such as Dragon, Blue Box, Sideshow Collectables and In The Past Toys, also seemed to focus exclusively on Third Reich subjects, and in 2002 they cancelled their 12-inch figure line. Since focusing on smaller scales, in 2014 21st Century Toys introduced a new action-figure brand, 'Ultimate Soldier XD', which, at 1:18 scale, was considerably smaller than traditional military action figures. However, the new scale at least had the advantage of being suit-

able for similarly scaled vehicles and large weapons systems to be more practically produced.

Sideshow Collectables started out in 1994. They originally created toy prototypes for major toy companies such as Mattel, Galoob and Wild Planet, but in 1999 began to market their own line of collectables, beginning with the 'Universal Classic Monsters' 8-inch action-figure licence, and then creating items in the more established 1:6-scale format that sold through speciality markets. At this time they also changed the suffix to their brand from 'toys' to 'collectables'.

Sideshow has forged collaborative relationships with Hollywood filmmakers and special-effect houses including Guillermo del Toro, Legacy Effects, Spectral Motion, Amalgamated Dynamics Inc. and KNB EFX to produce some of the most sought-after collectables from blockbuster films such as *Iron Man*, *The Transformers*, *The Avengers*, *Hellboy*, *Predators*, *Alien 3* and *Alien vs Predators*.

Sideshow Collectables is currently in partnership with Marvel, Disney, WB, Lucasfilm, DC, Blizzard Entertainment and others to create products from properties such as *The Marvel Universe*, *The DC Universe*, *Star Wars*, *Alien and Predator*, *Terminator*, *The Lord of the Rings*, *G.I. Joe*, *Halo*, *World of Warcraft*, *Star Craft II*, *Mass Effect 3*, *Diablo 3*, and many more.

Sideshow Collectables is also the exclusive distributor of Hot Toys' (see below) collectable figures in the United States, North and South America, Europe, Australia and throughout most Asian countries. With its headquarters in Kowloon, Hong Kong's Hot Toys Ltd was established in 2000 and began life concentrating solely on 1:6-scale military action figures. Since 2003, however, the company has branched out and secured licences and merchandising rights for a wide range of major movie products. These include *Avengers*, *Pirates of the Carib-*

Blue Box (BBI)
'Elite Force
Pearl Harbor
pilot' contents.

bean, *Bat Man: The Dark Knight*, *The Terminator*, *Alien* and *Superman* series, and a range of Hollywood legends including Marlon Brando, Sylvester Stallone, Bruce Lee and James Dean. Musicians such as Michael Jackson and Wong Ka Kui, founding member of the Hong Kong rock band, Beyond, have also been immortalized in 1:6-scale plastic by Hot Toys.

Going that extra mile to achieve scale realism, Hot Toys has secured patents for a couple of particularly clever innovations. One, the 'Parallel Eyeball Rolling System' (PERS), takes Palitoy's 'Eagle Eyes' to a new level. The other, 'The Interchangeable Faces Technique' (IFT), a component of its DX series, actually enables customers to change their action figure's expression: in seconds, a simple tool can alter Batman's demeanour from a square-jawed, no-nonsense grimace, to his trademark sardonic smile.

Hot Toys has complemented its 1:6 figures with a range

of large 1:4-scale figures and busts, a 'Movie Masterpiece Series' (MMS), a 'Power Pose' (PPS) series of predominantly 'Iron Man' characters as well as the sophisticated and consequently relatively expensive, 1:6-scale MMS diecast range

Established in 2003, the Hong Kong-based DID Corporation owns extensive manufacturing facilities in mainland China, where it produces its own figures (ODM: Own Development Manufacture), and products on behalf of other manufacturers such as Hasbro in the UK and Bandai in Japan (OEM: Original Equipment Manufacturer). DID is well known for producing excellent 12-inch military action figures from conflicts ranging from the Napoleonic Wars to World War II. Soldiers, samurai, fashion figures and movie characters all fall within DID's remit, accompanied by an extensive range of 1:6-scale vehicles and accessories, which even include tiny 1:6-scale leather shoes!

Immediately post-World War II, France's Mokarex began giving away 54mm plastic figures with their coffee. As tastes changed, Mokarex concentrated on coffee machines, but in 1963 Atelier de Gravure, the manufacturers of these fine premiums, founded the famous Historex Napoleonic figures range.

International toy manufacturers took full advantage of the post-war development aid on offer to mitigate the damage caused by the worldwide conflict, especially the financial support granted by the United States' Marshall Plan. Soon, grateful beneficiaries were investing in shiny new injection-moulding machines from manufacturers that included Arburg, Engel, Ferromatik and RH Windsor. Established companies such as America's Louis Marx and Britain's Lines Bros (parent of Tri-ang, Minic and Pedigree) were also quick to embrace such modern methods of toy production.

Ironically, those belligerents on the losing side often prospered most. With Germany at the heart of the Cold-War boundary between east and west, it was politically prudent for the Western democracies to bolster the fledgling Bundesrepublik, and consequently West Germany rose like a phoenix. In keeping with international practice, after World War II Japanese manufacturers also opted for injection

moulding, and many of their plants switched from traditional tinplate to the manufacture of polystyrene and polyethylene products.

Japan's initial resurgence wasn't as rapid as that of democratic West Germany, however. Exchange rate fluctuations, especially the readjustment following the United States' abandonment of the gold standard at the end of the 1960s, and its subsequent imposition of a 10 per cent surcharge on imported goods, made Japanese products increasingly expensive, and the nation's competitive growth faltered. Nevertheless, at least one south-east Asian country more than filled the void left by Nippon's absence, and by 1970 Hong Kong toy manufacturers were in the ascendant.

Hong Kong's Dominance in the Production of Plastic Toys

The Japanese invasion of China in 1937, and their

capture of Shanghai, had encouraged a wave of migration to Hong Kong. The Chinese civil war that followed Japan's surrender in 1945 further expedited the flow of refugees to the Crown Colony. Amongst those migrants were many industrialists bent on relocating there to take advantage of its relative freedoms and excellent logistics, such as Hong Kong's deep harbour (most suitable for merchant ships) and its established international airport. The fact that the territory's existing commercial and administrative infrastructure was based on tried and tested British legal practice was another perceived bonus.

Promptly, entrepreneurs such as Peter Chan Pui,

founder of Blue Box Toys, toy and model railway manufacturer Kader's Ting Hsiung-chao, and the entrepreneur Lam Leung-tim, known as 'LT', whose company Forward Winsome Industries expanded from the manufacture of a yellow plastic duck in 1948 – alleged to be Hong Kong's first plastic toy – began to spearhead the colony's dominance in the production of plastic toys. LT struck up an enduring friendship with Hasbro's Alan Hassenfield, which saw the licensed production of GI Joe and, later, 'Transformers'. By the late 1970s, Hong Kong had become synonymous with the production of plastic, especially toys such as action figures.

In 1971, Airfix used all sorts of plastic for both the figure and parachute canopy of their 'Skydiver', which, the box claimed, 'Goes up like a kite – comes down like a parachute'. I wonder how many really soared to 150 feet.

With everything established to encourage the adoption of new materials and high-speed methods of production, toy manufacturers worldwide eagerly embraced the new possibilities. Even well-established toy companies adapted production to suit this new environment. One of them, the Ideal Novelty and Toy Co., which had been founded in 1907 and can credibly claim to be the inventor of the teddy bear (see box), was one of the first manufacturers to produce a truly modern plastic doll when they introduced the 'Toni' series in 1949.

Their new doll was retailed as a joint promotion with the Toni Permanent Company, then a leading exponent of the permanent wave hairstyle. Since 1934, Ideal had enjoyed enormous success with its series of 'Shirley Temple' dolls, each of which featured a mohair wig of tumbling curly locks. The 'Toni' doll was equally popular, and little girls were encouraged to endlessly wash, comb, perm and style the doll's hair.

'Toni' came along at the right time and was able to take advantage of another new plastic, acrylonitrile butadiene styrene (ABS), which had only recently been added to the growing lexicon of plastics. ABS proved the perfect material for action figures. It was easy to mould and proved extremely robust, capable of withstanding any amount of roughhousing from excitable youngsters. Combined with the softer and more flexible PVC, developed some forty years previously and perfect for items such as capes, boots and shoes, belts, rifle slings and suchlike, ABS plastic was durable enough to survive the regular handling that resulted from endless outfit changes, and robust enough to survive almost anything other than the most damaging encounters with unyielding obstacles.

Ideal followed their 'Toni' doll in 1956 with 'Miss Revlon', which, as its name suggests, was another figure analogous to the world of beauty and cosmetics. 'Toni' and 'Miss Revlon' were enormously successful, but were soon to pale in comparison with the new girl on the block – and even though Ideal rushed out the short-lived clone 'Mitzi', they were unable to compete with Barbie, who arrived in 1959 and instantly overwhelmed the competition.

British Manufacturers

In Britain, doll manufacturers Rosebud, D.G. Todd & Co (whose pre-war composition 'Roddy Doll' resurfaced in hard plastic in 1957) and Alfred Pallet's Cascelloid Ltd (the forerunner of Palitoy) had long prevailed over others in the domestic toy doll market. Lines Bros was always hard on their heels, their Tri-ang brand possessing the largest toy factory in the world, a 750,000-square-feet establishment at Merton in Surrey. Tri-ang's Pedigree brand had long counted on girls as customers, its hard plastic dolls being hugely popular in Britain. But other than its 'Little Miss Vogue' range, even by the late 1950s its products were largely traditional and followed established lines, pursuing the trends rather than setting them.

The trendsetter was right around the corner.

AND ALONG CAME BARBIE

Ruth Handler noticed that her daughter Barbara didn't play with toy babies – she preferred her dolls to be dressed like adults, and when she played with them, her interaction mimicked the behaviour of grown-ups. Consequently, Ruth reckoned there might be a gap in the market – perhaps other young girls had a similar inclination. Fortunately, because her husband Elliot was a director of the Mattel toy company, she was in the unique position of being able to do some-thing about it.

However, when Ruth first proposed her idea to Mattel's management, Elliot and his colleagues didn't share her enthusiasm, and it wasn't until she discov-ered a German toy doll whilst on vacation in Europe that she resolved to pursue her idea further. With 'Bild Lilli' safe in her luggage, a doll with an adult figure that had been on sale since 1955 and matched her original concept, she went straight back to Mattel to show them what she envisaged. This time she was more successful.

Though not a comic-strip blonde bombshell like Lilli – a worldly-wise working girl who featured regu-larly in a popular comic strip in *Die Bild-Zeitung*, the popular daily tabloid – the doll that her husband's company committed itself to producing was still endowed with assets that Marilyn Monroe would have been proud of. She was guaranteed to stand out in every way.

Using 'Lilli' as a template, the doll that Mattel design engineer Jack Ryan finally came up with shared many of the original's features. Satisfied that they had found a winner, the prototype was given the green light, and Ruth named it Barbie, after her daughter Barbara.

The inspiration for Mattel co-founder Ruth Handler's Barbie, 'Bild Lilli' was launched on 12 August 1955 and produced until 1964. Its design was based on the comic-strip character 'Lilli', created by Reinhard Beuthien for the German tabloid *Bild*. During a visit to Germany in 1956, Ruth Handler thought 'Lilli' was exactly the type of doll that young American girls would play with.

MATTEL

Mattel, Inc. was founded in California in 1945, and since then its brands such as Fisher-Price, Barbie, Hot Wheels, Matchbox and Masters of the Universe have deservedly secured a position in the Fortune 500 for the business. Deriving its name from a combination of the surnames of founders Harold 'Matt' Matson and Elliot Handler, the business perhaps owes its fame mostly to Elliot's wife Ruth, creator of Barbie, the firm's most successful toy line. However, before the curvaceous doll's introduction in 1959, Mattel achieved its first success with 1947's 'Uke-A-Doodle', a toy ukulele that also doubled up as a music box. 'Turn Handle and it Plays Real Music – Two Toys in One!' promised the box art. Mattel also enjoys the honour of being the first commercial sponsor of the Mickey Mouse Club TV series in 1955.

In 1960 Mattel introduced 'Chatty Cathy', a talking doll that revolutionized the toy industry, and was followed by a flood of other pull-string talking dolls and toys that came on the market throughout the 1960s.

Mattel went public in 1960 and was listed on the New York Stock Exchange in 1963. Another enormous success, Hot Wheels, first appeared in 1968. In 1971 Mattel even spent $40 million buying 'The Ringling Bros' and 'Barnum & Bailey Circus' for $40 million from owners the Feld family.

Accounting difficulties in 1974 saw the Handlers leave the company. However, by 1975, under the stewardship of former vice president Arthur S. Spear, Mattel was back on track, and by 1977 was consistently achieving profits. In 1979 Mattel spent $12 million adding ownership of the 'Holiday on Ice' and 'Ice Follies' franchises to its entertainment portfolio.

Based on the stories of the heroic warrior 'He-Man' who battles against the evil lord 'Skeletor' and his armies of darkness for control of 'Castle Grayskull', the 'Masters of the Universe' toy line was one of Mattel's most successful action-figure ranges. At the time of writing, the author watched a mint-on-card (MOC) example of MOTU's 'Skeletor in Battle Armour' receive more than forty bids on eBay before selling for £1,210. Not bad for a figure dating from 1983!

MOTU, as it is known by fans, began life in 1982 with Mattel's release of the original 5½-inch action-figure series that was accompanied by a successful minicomics series, several children's books and subsequent editions of regular DC comics. Starring Dolph Lundgren and Frank Langella, in 1987 a Hollywood movie confirmed the popularity of MOTU amongst true fans, if not necessarily film critics, who panned the production. But when it comes to fantasy toys, what do the experts know?

Mattel purchased Fisher-Price Inc. in 1993, Tyco Toys Inc. in 1997, and Pleasant Company (maker of the 'American Girl' brand) in 1998, adding The Learning Company to its portfolio in 1999 for $3.5 billion.

In December 2000, Mattel sued the band Aqua, saying their song *Barbie Girl* violated the Barbie trademark and turned Barbie into a sex object, referring to her as a 'blonde bimbo'. The lawsuit was rejected in 2002.

Mattel 'Mork' and 'Mindy' action figures (1979).

Mattel 'Battlestar Galactica Commander Adama' (1978).

first animated project, 'Team Hot Wheels: The Origin of Awesome'. Further movies for Hot Wheels, 'Masters of the Universe', 'Monster High' and 'Max Steel' are in production. The same year, *Fortune* magazine claimed that Mattel was one of the top one hundred companies to work for, with more than a thousand of the business's employees having worked there for longer than fifteen years.

In 2014 Mattel purchased Canadian company Mega Brands Inc., creators of the famous Mega Bloks construction toy. In 2016, with incumbent Hasbro's licence due to expire the following year, Mattel acquired the licence for Jurassic Park toys from NBC Universal. In 2017 a takeover deal from Hasbro fell through when Mattel rejected the offer.

In 2018 the dramatic liquidation of Toys "R" Us sent shock waves through the entire toy industry and forced Mattel to lay off more than 2,000 employees. The same year, mandated to make movies based on the firm's products, Mattel Films was formed. 2019 also saw the company launch the world's first range of gender-neutral dolls, branded Creatable World.

In 2002, Mattel closed its last factory in the United States, which had originally been part of Fisher-Price, and instead, in an effort to reduce costs, outsourced their production to China. However, because of quality control considerations and a scandal involving lead contamination in 2007, Mattel were forced to recall over eighteen million products. This was followed by the recall of more than seven million 'Polly Pocket' toys, over half a million 'Barbies' and countless other toys, and resulted in Mattel being fined $2.9 million by the Consumer Products Safety Commission for marketing, importing and selling non-compliant toys.

In 2010 HIT Entertainment licensed Thomas & Friends toy lines to Mattel. The close working relationship resulted in Mattel purchasing HIT in 2011 for $680 million.

In October 2013, Mattel launched its new in-house film studio, Playground Productions, and produced its

Mattel 'Avatar Neytiri' action figure (2009).

Before young girls played with fashion dolls such as Barbie, and 'Lilli' before her, they were expected to be satisfied with traditional dolls such as this 'I am a Baby Rosebud Doll' from the early nineteen-fifties.

ing the number of 'Barbies' sold each year, in March 2009 they announced that three dolls were sold each second, and it is estimated that well over a billion Barbie dolls have been sold worldwide, in over 150 countries.

Barbie Takes the World by Storm

Mattel's enormous success with Barbie took its competitors by surprise, and as Louis Marx had tried with 'its' Lilli, many others attempted to grab part of the action. Indeed, quite swiftly after Barbie's debut, Canada's L. Davis Textiles Company (Davtex), a firm specializing in producing clone dolls in Hong Kong for sale in Canada and North America, released its look-alike 'Denise', 'Suzette', 'Michelle' and 'Diane' dolls. New York-based Fab-Lu even rushed out one called 'Babs – The Teenage Fashion Doll', which joined a growing suite of figures known as 'Hong Kong Lillis'. Goldberger Toys brought their 'Miss Babette' doll to market, and the Valentine Toy Company Inc. had a lookalike of their own, called 'Polly'.

As we have seen, by the mid-1950s developments in production, especially in the field of plastic injection moulding, meant that it was now easy to manufacture inexpensive but very robust dolls. But more importantly, instead of being offered only baby or infant dolls, little girls could now choose an up-to-the-minute teenage fashion doll that reflected the real world and met their aspirations – exceeded them in fact. Barbie was what little girls had always wanted – they just hadn't realized it until Ruth Handler's doll made it manifest.

Barbie made her debut at the American International Toy Fair in New York on 9 March 1959, and within a year nearly a third of a million were sold.

Louis Marx & Co subsequently acquired the rights to 'Lilli', and in March 1961 sued Mattel for copyright infringement. Mattel counter-sued, and the matter was settled out of court in 1963. In 1964 Mattel finally acquired the rights to the 'Bild Lilli' doll themselves, and saw to it that production of the Fräulein ceased.

While Mattel won't release an exact figure regard-

But it was the larger, more established companies that felt most threatened. In 1961 the Louis Marx Company introduced its range of 'Miss Seventeen' dolls, which, although they were 'Bild Lilli' clones, were much larger than Barbie. Obviously concerned to avoid copying Mattel's creation too closely, they followed these up with a 7½-inch doll with the not-very-American moniker 'Miss Marlene': perhaps named after Lili Marleen, 'the girl under the lantern', this might have been a nod towards their German precursors. By the early 1960s, Plastic Molded Arts, another American company, founded in 1949, appeared less inhibited, flooding the toy shops with their 12-inch 'Lilly' dolls.

LOUIS MARX

American toymaker and businessman Louis Marx was born in 1896. By the 1950s Louis Marx and Company was the largest toy company in the world. Often known as 'the Henry Ford of the toy industry', Marx had served in the US Army during World War I, and his passion and interest for the military endured until his death in 1982 – one of the consequences being that Marx always included plenty of 'war toys' in the catalogues.

Marx began his career with Ferdinand Strauss, a manufacturer of mechanical toys, but in 1919 he left, and in partnership with his brother David, founded the toy company that bore their surname. Soon afterwards he managed to acquire some of the machine tools and patterns from Strauss's now defunct company (I wonder if Ferdinand regretted allowing his young apprentice to leave), releasing his former mentor's toys under the Marx brand. By 1926 Louis Marx was a millionaire – not bad for a man who had left the army as a sergeant.

Louis Marx and Company employed modern methods of mass production, but also thriftily reused existing tools and patterns, repurposing current moulds with the simplest modifications to produce 'new' toys – some venerable toy-train tooling from the early 1930s, for example, allegedly remained in production until 1972.

Unlike those of most other companies, Marx's revenues grew during the Great Depression, and against the trend of a time when banks were foreclosing and manufacturers were obliged to decommission plant, the business established new production facilities in economically hard-hit industrial areas, most notably in Pennsylvania.

Marx also quickly established himself overseas, developing manufacturing capability in England. By 1937, the company had assets of more than $3.2 million.

Louis Marx toured Europe as a special consultant at the end of World War II, advising on new methods of toy manufacturing and helping foreign toy companies deal with the rigours of reconstruction. The network-ing that naturally resulted proved enormously valuable, and Marx carefully employed the contacts he had made to forge business partnerships and open new factories in Europe and Japan. By the 1950s the Marx Company had twelve factories worldwide. In 1955, a *Time* magazine article proclaimed Louis Marx as the 'Toy King', and that year the company enjoyed sales of around $50 million.

Marx's toys included tinplate buildings, tin toys, toy soldiers, playsets, toy dinosaurs, mechanical toys, toy guns, action figures, dolls, dolls' houses, toy cars and trucks, the famous 'Rock'em, Sock'em' robots, and the iconic 'Big Wheel' tricycle (now enshrined in the National Toy Hall of Fame). Marx's more expensive toys were supplemented by a variety of cheaper HO-scale and O-scale trains, and a range of inexpensive toys were sold in dime stores.

Marx figure playsets will be eternally popular with enthusiasts, but throughout the 1960s and 1970s their numerous compendiums based both on television shows and real historical events proved especially popular. These included classics such as 'Roy Rogers' Rodeo Ranch and Western Town', Walt Disney's 'Davy Crockett at the Alamo', 'Gunsmoke', 'Wagon Train' and 'The Battle of the Little Big Horn'. In the early 1960s Marx even produced a dolls' house with a bomb shelter to ensure that youngsters embraced the principles of 'Duck and Cover' – the US equivalent of Britain's 'Protect and Survive'.

In 1963, Marx notably capitalized on the beatnik craze, releasing a series of whacky plastic figurines called the 'Nutty Mads'. These 'far out' toys were designed to compete with kit company Revell, who were enjoying tremendous success with the kits they licensed from custom-car king, Big Daddy Ed Roth and Hawk Models, who had hit gold turning illustrator Bill Campbell's fantastic creations into a range of automobile mutations that far predated 'Transformers' – the inimitable 'Weird-ohs'.

Louis Marx retired in 1972, selling his company to Quaker Oats for $54 million.

Hardest hit, however, was toy giant Hasbro, which had struck gold in the 1950s with their 'Mr Potato Head' toy, and were now a major Disney licence holder. Founded in Providence, Rhode Island, in 1923, the Hassenfeld Brothers watched as Barbie cleaned up. They had nothing like it – a toy for which owners continually purchased additional accessory

Mattel introduced 'Midge', Barbie's best friend, in 1963. With a fuller, more childlike face, Midge was partly introduced to counter some of the criticisms of Barbie's unrealistic body shape.

When Barbie burst on the scene in 1959, she was an immediate success. Out went the babies and bath-time scenarios, and in came sassiness and the catwalk. So successful was she that Hasbro, who had been perched at the top of the US toy tree, suddenly felt very insecure. Could something similar be done with a boys' toy?

sets. However, they immediately set about looking for a product that did what Barbie did, but for boys rather than girls. As we shall see, GI Joe (Action Man) was the result – and the action-figure genre was born.

Mattel had been a sponsor of the Mickey Mouse Club television programme since 1955, becoming the first toy company to broadcast commercials to children. They used this medium to promote Barbie, and by 1961 the enormous consumer demand for the doll encouraged Mattel to introduce a boyfriend for Barbie. Handler named him Ken, after her son. Barbie's best friend, 'Midge', came out in 1963, while her little sister, Skipper, made her debut the following year.

Thus Ruth Handler's idea for a doll that was anything but infantile proved a storming success, and Barbie went on to underpin Mattel's future progress. The company went public in 1960, and was listed on the New York Stock Exchange in 1963. Throughout the sixties, Mattel commenced an acquisition spree, purchasing established giants such as Britain's Rosebud Dolls, and the famous US construction kit company Monogram.

Soon after they released Barbie, Mattel introduced another hugely successful doll, 'Chatty Cathy'. A 'pull-string' doll that talked, 'Chatty Cathy' was second only to Barbie in terms of sales.

Competition for Barbie

Apart from direct copies from smaller manufacturers desperately trying to emulate Mattel's success, other larger and more established manufacturers, all careful to avoid litigation for plagiarism, designed and produced their own, more fashionable dolls that were more likely to appeal to teenage girls than the traditional infant dolls. By 1963, British manufacturer Pedigree's 'Sindy' doll was in the shops. All was all right until the late 1970s when Hasbro bought the rights to Sindy and remodelled her face to better suit the

Purchasers were encouraged to join 'The Sindy Set' and not only acquire the eponymous heroine, but also 'Mitzi', her French friend, and her boyfriend 'Paul'.

A subsidiary of Lines Bros, Britain's Pedigree Dolls & Toys introduced 'Sindy', their answer to Barbie, in 1963.

The US's American Character Doll Company also decided to try for some of Barbie's market share, and in 1963 introduced 'Tressy', the doll with the hair that magically grew. This is 'Toots', Tressy's sister.

US market, something they quickly rectified when Mattel slapped a lawsuit on them.

The same year that Sindy made her debut in Britain, back across the pond another teenage doll, 'Tressy', initially released by the American Character Doll Company but later by Ideal Toys, gave Barbie a real run for her money. With hair that magically grew longer, or once it was wound back into her head became shorter, Tressy was a revelation. The doll also proved a huge success in Europe.

Mattel Riding High

In 1968, Mattel rounded off its decade of success with the release of Hot Wheels racing cars, which raced along a special interconnecting plastic track that could be formed into vertiginous slopes and even bent into loops. Until 1997 when Mattel bought Tyco Toys, Hot Wheels was the main competitor to Matchbox. By acquiring Tyco, which by then owned Matchbox, Mattel had the monopoly over the world of 1:64-scale diecasts.

After suffering from breast cancer, in 1974 Ruth Handler left Mattel, and her husband Elliot did so shortly afterwards. In 1989 the couple became the first living inductees to the US Toy Industry Hall of Fame. Ruth died in 2002, followed by Elliot in 2011.

By the mid-1980s, the success of 'My Little Pony' and 'Transformers' helped Hasbro overtake Mattel again to become the world's largest toy company. Positions reversed in the 1990s, after Mattel added Fisher-Price to their holdings and were in turn propelled to the top spot in the toy industry. Indeed, riding high, in 1996 Mattel even tried to settle things once and for all when it attempted to purchase Hasbro for $5.2 billion. The offer was quickly withdrawn after Hasbro made it clear that they had no intention of selling.

At the turn of the twenty-first century, Mattel emerged as the leading manufacturer of children's toys, capturing 12 per cent of the global market. Together with Barbie and Hot Wheels, Mattel's stable also included other famous brands such as American Girl and, of course, Matchbox.

Changing Times

The amazing accession of social media and the variety of smartphones and tablets required to access the numerous platforms available, all of which have conspired to lure youngsters away from traditional playthings, has meant that in recent years time-honoured toys such as dolls have failed to entertain young girls in the way they used to, and as a consequence Mattel has struggled to impress investors. In November 2017 *The Wall Street Journal* even reported that it was Hasbro's turn to try to acquire its major competitor. At the time it was worth $11 billion, when Mattel was valued at a more modest $5 billion. Five days later, Reuters reported that Mattel had rejected the offer. Doubtless this game of financial ping pong will continue.

Indeed, in January 2018 CNN Money.com reported that the 'Hasbro-Mattel merger rumor just won't die,' adding, 'even though Hasbro has done better than Mattel lately, Wall Street is concerned that plans by bankrupt Toys "R" Us to close more than 180 US stores will hurt both toymakers.'

Changing times haven't helped the Barbie brand much, either. Over the years, although generating huge sales, she's been responsible for a lot of controversy, too. Despite having a series of very credible jobs, from airline stewardess, doctor, pilot and astronaut to Olympic athlete – and on one occasion even US presidential candidate – critics argue that Barbie's eternal passion for designer outfits, cars, and her aspiration to live in a 'dream house', have encouraged children to be materialistic rather than altruistic. In an increasingly politically correct world, parents encourage their children to share, not to covet.

But above all, it is perhaps Barbie's striking physique that has repeatedly been at odds with parents. Her tiny waist and ample bosom – it is estimated that if she were a real woman, her measurements would be 36-18-38 – have led many to claim that Barbie provided little girls with an unrealistic role model and only served to foster negative body images.

Following the departure of Margo Georgiadis, Mattel's CEO who had only been with the company for fourteen months before joining Google, *Bloom-*

berg Opinion's Sarah Halzack wrote: 'Mattel Inc. seems to change CEOs about as quickly as kids cycle through favorite toys.'

In April 2018, Margo Georgiadis was replaced by Ynon Kreiz, who became the fourth captain of Mattel's ship since 2015, a sign of the tough times and the dwindling demand for traditional favourites such as Barbie and her stablemate toys from Fisher-Price: 'Bob the Builder' and 'Dora the Explorer'. Kreiz is eminently qualified for this role: with a previous glowing career in children's television – in 1996 he launched 'Fox Kids Europe' in partnership with Rupert Murdoch's 'News Corporation' – he then served as Chairman and CEO of Netherlands-based digital production company Endemol, before joining the board of Makers Studios, the Los Angeles-based multi-channel network, who, amongst other things, produce short-form videos for YouTube and other platforms. With this record Kreiz understands modern tastes and trends better than most.

Perhaps there is another Barbie waiting around the corner to revive the fortunes of this American giant.

Barbie badge.

'A DOLL FOR BOYS!': GI JOE, THE US FIGHTING MAN

Three brothers, Herman, Hillel and Henry Hassenfeld, founded Hasbro in 1923. Back then, the company was called Hassenfeld Brothers, and transacted business as a distributor of fabric remnants. Ingeniously, three years later the brothers used these remnants for fabric-covered pencil boxes, which they marketed and sold successfully. Gradually they found other uses for such decorated containers, and soon the contents within began to include assorted toys and novelties. One of the most successful sets included a collection of miniatures of the kind of equipment used by nurses and doctors. After using such outfits, following every successful medical intervention on their dolls and teddies, once these budding Florence Nightingales had packed away their brightly coloured Hassenfeld Brothers toy suitcases, in recognition of their accomplishments they might award themselves a diploma from the 'Toyville Nurse College'.

Hasbro's Dedicated Toy Division

It appeared that good business could be had in the field of fun and games, and it therefore didn't take long for the Hassenfeld Brothers to decide to establish a dedicated toy division. By the 1950s their decision had proved to be right on the money, literally, because by then Hasbro was behind one of the most successful toys in US history – 'Mr Potato Head'.

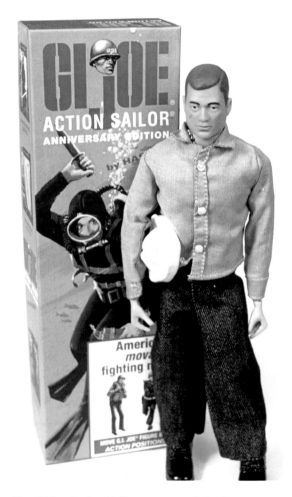

The GI Joe Action Sailor was one of the few figures that was good to go straight from the box. Disappointingly to many purchasers, most boxed figures required the purchase of numerous accessories before they were fit for purpose.

Soon young Americans were choosing from a huge variety of 'Mr Potato Head' options. There was 'Oscar Orange', 'Katie Carrot', 'Cooky the Cucumber', 'Frankie Frank' with his friend 'Mr Mustard Head', and even 'Jumpin Mr Potato Head' with spring-loaded feet – 'Wind him up and watch him go'. When their 'Mr Potato Head' commercial aired in 1952, Hasbro made history by being the first company to embrace the power of television to promote a toy.

The enormous success of Hassenfeld Bros' 'Mr Potato Head' range meant that by 1954 Hasbro had become a Disney major licensee.

Mr Potato Head's lengthy hegemony was finally challenged in 1959 with the advent of Barbie. Not surprisingly, a glamorous fashion doll had greater appeal for teenage girls than a plastic tuber, and arch-rival Mattel was suddenly propelled to dizzy heights. Mattel's co-founder, Elliot Handler, often said that a key ingredient to Barbie's success was that they had found a toy that adhered to the shaving razor business model – the razor is just the start, the real money is in the subsequent consumables, the razor blades, which unavoidably become regular purchases. With the accession of disposable razors, I suppose the nearest equivalents today are printing ink cartridges.

Little more than a miniature plastic mannequin, Barbie became the clothes horse for an infinite variety of outfits and accessories. Each new ensemble was eagerly awaited and readily snapped up when available by her growing band of fans. Nothing else on the market came close to offering young girls the same play value as the bountiful Barbie – she had a get-up for every occasion. Hasbro needed to find something similar.

Despite being envious of Mattel's achievement with Barbie, Hasbro was far too well established and business savvy to risk exposing itself to accusations

GI Joe's 1964 debut in the United States was nothing short of sensational. The scar on his cheek wasn't only there to make him look macho, it was a cunning copyright protection device.

of copy-cat behaviour. It was clear that older children had become less willing to play with traditional toys and were more inclined towards modern pursuits and pastimes than ever before. Barbie encouraged young girls to mimic the behaviour and fashion choices of adults, inspiring them to curate ever-growing collections of outfits and accessories. Surely boys would embrace a toy aimed specifically at them with the same gusto. Hasbro certainly hoped so.

HASBRO

In 1923, in Providence, the capital of Rhode Island in the New England region of the USA, the three Hassenfeld brothers, Hillel, Herman and Henry, founded their eponymous company. Their business began by selling textile remnants, but soon expanded into the lucrative field of school supplies. With the cost of pencils rising, the brothers decided to cut out the middleman and instead, manufacture their own products. This was a wise decision, which delivered reliable income that could be reinvested in their business. In 1940 Hassenfeld Bros branched out again and started manufacturing such disparate items as children's doctor and nurses' compendiums and modelling clay; by 1942 toys were their exclusive focus.

Hillel died in 1943 and Henry Hassenfeld became CEO, with his son, Merrill, becoming president. The advent of plastic injection moulding during the 1940s proved an ideal process for toy production, and Hassenfeld took full advantage of the new process.

In 1949 inventor George Lerner created a toy first called 'Make a Face', which he initially sold to a cereal company who packaged a range of plastic features such as eyes, noses and ears in their boxes: when removed, these could be pushed into fruits or vegetables – eventually potatoes became the most popular choice to use as a base. In 1951 Lerner bought it back off the cereal company and struck a better deal with Hassenfeld Bros, who in turn revamped the product and changed the name to 'Mr Potato Head'.

Mr Potato Head was the first toy to be advertised on American television, and was an immediate success; it secured Hassenfeld Bros' future until they hit the jackpot with GI Joe in 1964. A 12-inch action figure, this offering was an immediate sensation, and during its inaugural year accounted for two-thirds of the company's sales. The business changed its name to Hasbro Industries in 1968.

Subsequent to the huge success of GI Joe, Hasbro's story is littered with milestones. In 1969 Hasbro launched its successful 'Romper Room' range of pre-school products. Aiming at a demographic that was only a few years older, in 1982 the company unveiled its enormously successful 'My Little Pony' toy line.

Hasbro *Stargate* figures (1994).

Hasbro *Jurassic Park* action figure of Dennis Nedry, the disaffected programming whizz kid behind the computer system in the park (1993).

Hasbro *Planet of the Apes* 'Major Leo Davidson', the astronaut leader of the human rebellion, and 'Colonel Attar', commander of the Ape Armies, action figures (2001).

The Playskool Institute was originally established by Lucille King in Milwaukee, Wisconsin in 1928, and became a division of a major lumber company there. Following some further business developments, by 1940 it had become the Playskool Manufacturing Company, and in 1943 added 'Lincoln Logs', the famous educational toy invented by John, second son of architect Frank Lloyd Wright, to its inventory. In 1968 Playskool became a subsidiary of toy company Milton Bradley, which in 1984 was acquired by Hasbro, ending 124 years of family ownership; for a short period the new company Hasbro Bradley was the largest toy company in the USA. That same year Hasbro enjoyed further massive success with the launch of the 'Transformers' toy line. In 1985 Hasbro changed its name again, from Hasbro Bradley to Hasbro Inc.

In 1991 Hasbro acquired 'Play-Doh', following the decision of the previous owner General Mills to pull out of the toy and hobby business. 'Play-Doh' is a product

(continued overleaf)

HASBRO *(continued)*

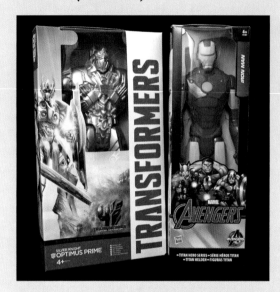

Hasbro 'Iron Man and Transformers', and 'Optimus Prime' (2018).

with its origins in the 1930s, when Cincinnati-based soap manufacturer Kutol Products developed the putty-like material for use as a wallpaper cleaner. In the 1990s Hasbro also streamlined its games output (it had acquired Parker Brothers when it purchased MB), and went on to purchase the Tonka Corporation and Kenner Products, with whom they unleashed 'Furbies' upon an unexpected world, together with many other enormously successful franchises. In 1998, Hasbro made two very significant acquisitions: first, the long-established strategic war-games publisher Avalon Hill for $6 million, and the toy company Galoob for $220 million.

For Hasbro the twenty-first century was character-ized by a great deal of restructuring, including some issues about its environmental policies, and about the behaviour and employment policies of its overseas suppliers, notably in China.

In 2014, it was said that Hasbro was back on the acquisition trail and about to purchase DreamWorks Animation, but after much excited speculation, the talks were reported to have fallen through.

On 10 November 2017, the *Wall Street Journal* claimed

that Hasbro had made a takeover offer for Mattel, Inc. At the time, Mattel was worth $5 billion, while Hasbro's value stood at $11 billion. Five days later, however, Reuters reported that Mattel had rejected the offer.

In February 2018, Saban Brands granted Hasbro rights to 'Power Rangers', the hugely popular concept created by Haim Saban and launched in 1993 as 'Mighty Morphin Power Rangers'. Initially this made them a global master toy licensee, with the offer of an option to purchase the franchise outright in future.

Several other licensing agreements based on Hasbro products followed. These included the Monopoly Mansion Hotel, a luxury hotel concept based on the famous board game, the first of which was scheduled to open in Kuala Lumpur, Malaysia, and the NERF Action Xperience family entertainment centre, a concept featuring NERF activity zones and merchandizing stores, as well as food and beverage areas; this was premiered in Singapore and is due to be launched in the USA in late 2020. As well as the above, Hasbro is also developing a range of other theme parks and resorts.

Hasbro, *Raiders of the Lost Ark* 'Indiana Jones' action figure (2008).

Hasbro's New Toy Line

Whilst they might not have been too concerned about the clothes adult men wore, young boys undoubtedly admired the achievements of those who had served in the armed forces and with World War II less than two decades away, many of their familial relatives, fathers and older brothers were veterans. Some kinsfolk had probably been in the military more recently: the Korean war had ended less than a decade before, and Hasbro was keen to develop a new toy line that would tap into the zeitgeist, offering something that would appeal to boys in the same way that Barbie had with girls. Girls might aspire to the catwalk, but many boys aspired to the field of battle.

A soldier figure was the obvious choice of subject. The result, of course, would be GI Joe, the precise genesis of which is still subject to debate, although in spite of this its development has become the stuff of legend. There is no doubt, however, that three men, namely Larry Reiner, Stan Weston and Don Levine, were the progenitors of this fabulously successful toy.

Established custom has it that during a brainstorming meeting about their successful Tammy doll line, Larry Reiner, a designer with the Ideal Toy Company that owned the product, proposed the idea of Tammy having a range of male relatives. It was suggested that Tammy's father could be a fireman; perhaps her uncle might be a policeman?

Larry preferred the idea of a soldier character, and following the meeting mentioned this to his boss, Lionel Weintraub, who allegedly responded with the infamous pronouncement, 'Boys will never play with a doll!' This version of the story concludes with Reiner mentioning his idea to another toy designer, Stanley Weston, during a meeting with him at the 1963 Toy Fair.

At the time, Weston, proprietor of New York's Weston Merchandizing Corp, had already been thinking of an articulated military figure of the same scale as Barbie, which could be tied in with Gene Roddenberry's new television series, *The Lieutenant* (*Star Trek* was still a few years off). Weston took the idea to Hassenfeld executive Don Levine, but he didn't like the notion of licensing a toy to the new television

To get the 'GI Joe Action Pilot' to look anything like he did on the box required the purchase of all these accessory sets.

series. As it turned out, Levine's lack of enthusiasm was fortuitous because *The Lieutenant* only ran for a single season, and is now largely forgotten, unlike Roddenberry's next big idea, *Star Trek*. Nevertheless, Levine was very enthusiastic about the idea of a scale soldier figure that could support a wide range of accurate uniforms, and perhaps have access to larger accessories such as jeeps and artillery pieces.

The day following their meeting Weston wrote to thank Don Levine for his time. In the letter he said: 'I very much enjoyed our meeting in New York yesterday, and I'm especially pleased you felt our comprehensive military-combat new product idea might be something for a future Hassenfeld line.' He also listed the key essentials of the new toy, saying that the central component, the figure itself, should be a 'rugged-looking scale doll for boys', and should come complete with a 'military wardrobe to scale, military headgear to scale and military weapons to scale.'

Enthused by Levine's initial reaction to his concept, Weston rushed back to his offices to build a prototype of his new figure, even splashing out $52 of his own cash at a local craft store for the materials he required to construct it. The resulting prototype, with carefully hand-painted face complete with five-o'clock shadow and brown hair, was constructed over wire armatures and consisted of a combination of hand-fashioned plastic and metal components, all clothed in a hand-sewn olive-green uniform. In the crook of his right arm the prototype figure supported a regulation issue camouflaged US M1 helmet.

Because he feared a similar response from his boss to that of Ideal's Lionel Weintraub, Don Levine scheduled Weston's next presentation to coincide with a time when Merrill Hassenfeld was out of the country. He also forbade any use of the word 'doll' in association with his new war toy, insisting instead on the substitution of the now legendary term 'action figure'.

The Action Figure Is Born

Weston's action-figure maquette was a resounding success. Everyone at Hassenfeld Bros loved it, including Merrill when he returned from business overseas. Even though by 1963 his company wasn't turning in the numbers it had so reliably posted in earlier years, it was Merrill Hassenfeld who finally confirmed the success of the toy that was to become GI Joe and in turn Action Man, making available the funding needed to develop it. Merrill Hassenfeld is acknowledged as the critical fourth man in the genesis of the action-figure story, and it was he who secured the considerable finance required to cover the cost of tooling, mould-making and manufacturing for what would be a very complicated toy with as many as twenty-six articulated parts.

Part of the initial outlay that Hassenfeld raised was

required to buy out Weston's concept. Levine had offered a choice of a small sales royalty in perpetuity, or a one-time payment of $75,000. Weston countered and asked for $100,000 – a huge sum in 1963, which he received, but which was a fraction of what he would have earned if he had opted for a percentage.

But Stanley Weston wasn't done with action figures, and after agreeing to the deal with Hassenfeld Bros (they didn't change their name to Hasbro until 1968, but for ease we will use this label from now on) he took the idea of a new 12-inch articulated figure for boys to the Ideal Toy Company. This time Weston proposed 'Captain Magic', an action hero who could adopt the guise of whichever champion was best suited to solve the challenge at hand. Ingeniously, all the super-heroes Weston suggested were represented by his own company, Leisure Concepts.

After finishing with GI Joe, Stanley Weston wasn't done with action figures, and took the idea of a new 12-inch articulated figure for boys to Ideal. Originally named 'Captain Magic', in 1966 Ideal changed his name to 'Captain Action'. The figure is now quite rare. Disappointing sales meant that after just two years, in 1968 Ideal Toys discontinued it.

IDEAL TOYS

Russian-born businessman and inventor Morris Michtom and his wife Rose founded the Ideal Toy and Novelty company in 1907, and at one time it went on to become the largest doll manufacturer in the USA. Fascinatingly, their company was born of the success of the teddy bear, the endearing plush keepsake inspired by a cartoon revealing American president Theodore Roosevelt's compassion for a bear he had cornered and held within his sights at the end of an unsuccessful hunting trip in Mississippi in 1902.

Mint-in-Box Ideal Toys 'Evel Knievel' figure (1977).

After seeing the cartoon, Michtom created his own plush bear cub, which he sent to Roosevelt. Receiving permission to use Roosevelt's name, Michtom put an example of the bear in his shop window, next to a sign saying 'Teddy's Bear'. At the same time in Germany, Steiff, home of the famous 'button ear' bears, produced their own stuffed bear inspired by the same incident. After exhibiting their version at the Leipzig Toy Fair, it was subsequently retailed in the USA.

Allegedly unaware of each other's efforts, both Steiff and Michtom manufactured 'Teddy's Bears' at around the same time, and to this day, exactly who was first remains a mystery. However, Michtom undeniably got his into the shops in the USA before Steiff, and this was the catalyst for the formation of the Ideal Toy and Novelty company a few years afterwards.

One of Ideal's longest-lasting products was 'Betsy Wetsy', a doll whose first name was the same as the daughter of Abraham Katz, who would soon become the head of the company. Betsy Wetsy's surname referred to the fact that after being given a drink, she would wet her nappy! Introduced in 1934, this doll was the first of a kind, and was so successful – numerous other doll manufacturers quickly made dolls that also wet themselves – that it remained in production for more than fifty years. Making its debut in 1934, the 'Shirley Temple Doll' was another of their best-selling dolls. Ideal follow this with licensed Disney dolls and a 'Judy Garland Doll'.

After Michtom's death in 1938, the company changed its name to the Ideal Toy Company, and Michtom's nephew Abraham Katz, father of the original Betsy, became chief executive. Ideal grew exponentially during World War II, its stock value increasing from $2 million to $11 million. Success also continued post-war, with Ideal selling its products under licence in Canada, Australia, the United Kingdom and Brazil.

Post-war, two cosmetics-based doll series were launched. 'Toni' was introduced at the end of the 1940s, produced in association with Toni Home Permanent, a market leader in the US permanent-wave

(continued overleaf)

IDEAL TOYS *(continued)*

Ideal Toys *CHiPs* 'Ponch' figure (1981).

Ideal acquired the defunct company's mould tools, patents and trademarks. As part of the purchase they also obtained 'Tressy', the doll with the magically flourishing hair.

In late 1971, Ideal joined the New York Stock Exchange and was valued at $71 million, when it was recognized as one of the USA's top three toy companies.

Popular Ideal toys in the 1970s included a range of 'Evel Knievel' toys, 'Snoopy' toys, and the 'Tuesday Taylor' and 'Wake-up Thumbelina' dolls. However, by the late 1970s Ideal experienced the ups and downs to be expected of the toy trade, making $3.7 million in fiscal year 1979–1980, but losing $15.5 million during 1980–1981.

The first toy company to retail a genuine Rubik's Cube, in May 1981 Ideal filed civil suits against dozens of distributors and retailers in an attempt to stop the sale of knock-off cubes. Then in 1982 the CBS/Columbia Group, which already owned the Gabriel Industries toy division, acquired Ideal on the strength of its Rubik's Cube business, paying $58 million for the privilege; but in 1987 it decided to sell Ideal to Viewmaster International.

No sooner that the ink on the contract was dry, a new entity, View-Master Ideal emerged. In 1989, View-Master Ideal was in turn bought by Tyco Toys, the Ideal line remaining part of Tyco until Tyco's merger with Mattel, Inc. in 1997. Ideal's United Kingdom assets had been sold to Hasbro, which subsequently released 'Mouse Trap' and 'KerPlunk' under its MB Games brand.

Following the May 2013 acquisition of Alex Toys by Propel Equity Partners, in January 2014 the Ideal brand became part of a new company, Alex Brands.

hairstyling business. In 1956 Ideal introduced 'Miss Revlon', another fashion doll, but this time one that was linked to the Revlon Cosmetics Company. 'Miss Revlon' came in 18-inch, 20-inch and substantial 23-inch sizes. Not surprisingly, 'Little Miss Revlon' was smaller, standing just 10½ inches tall.

In 1951, Ideal went into partnership with competitors the American Character Doll Company and the Alexander Doll Company, and established the United States-Israeli Toy and Plastic Corporation, manufacturing toys in Israel and the USA. But in 1968 the American Character Doll Company filed for bankruptcy, and

When first marketed by Ideal in 1966, Captain Magic's name was changed to 'Captain Action'. But name change or no name change, nothing could improve sales, which declined steadily from the figure's introduction; after just two years, in 1968 Ideal Toys discontinued it. In fact so brief was Captain Action's existence that surviving original figures, outfits and accessories today command the highest prices on the collectors' market.

Thirty years after Captain Action's demise, retro toy company Playing Mantis revived the licence and he returned, but even this iteration of the action figure only survived for a couple of years. Since 2005 Captain Action Enterprises have held the licence for the product, and have busily produced a range of items from toys to trading cards and even clothing. In 2013 US company Round 2 released a version of 'Captain Action' for the twenty-first century. This has proved a boon to collectors, who have been paying a king's ransom for original 'Captain Action' figures and accessories. Indeed, at the time of writing I saw an original 1966 vintage mint-in-box Ideal Toys figure listed on eBay for £499!

The Development of GI Joe

Now back to the story about the development of what was to become GI Joe. Although the soldier figure had received the green light from management, it was still without a name, a brand, or even a preliminary packaging style. To remedy this shortcoming, Levine selected a small team consisting of Jerry Einhorn, Sam Speers and Janet Downing, and tasked them with taking his nascent action figure to the next level.

Initially it was thought that each of the different characters – soldier, sailor and airman – should have an individual name. 'Rocky', 'Skip' and 'Ace', respectively, were early favourites considered by the study group during this development stage. To contain each of the trio of miniature fighting men, Hasbro's studio also designed brightly illustrated boxes, each of which featured a representation of the character

DC Comics licensed the character from Ideal and published five issues of 'Captain Action' in 1968. This is the second edition.

inside, fully attired in combat gear and in a dramatic action pose.

Janet Downing was a staff artist there, and after hearing that the company's advertisers felt that a single, over-arching name would make marketing the toy much easier, she proposed GI Joe. The initials G and I were shorthand for 'Government Issue' or 'General Issue', and were as familiar to twentieth-century US citizens as are the letters W and D for War Department (accompanied by a broad arrow and used to mark government property) for those of us in the United Kingdom. In 1945 American General Dwight D. Eisenhower famously said that 'the truly heroic figure of this war is GI Joe and his counterparts in the air, the navy, and the Merchant Marine of every one of the United Nations'.

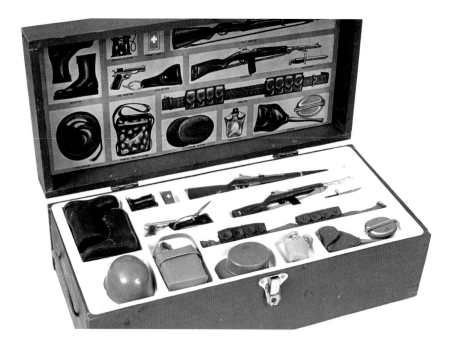

As the number of accessories amassed by avid enthusiasts continued to grow, it was fortunate that Hasbro produced a useful 'Footlocker' in which to store them.

Until the new product was launched, however, the appellation GI Joe was known to only a very few at Hasbro, and the programme was shielded in secrecy to prevent it leaking and enabling competitors to rush something similar to market before the company could complete the enormous logistic task of tooling, manufacturing, assembling and packaging the myriad components of their own figure. Until that day the new product was referred to only as 'the robot', and employees were warned that if news leaked to competitors such as Mattel, Marx or Ideal they would forfeit their jobs.

'The sales force was forbidden to use the term "doll" – if anyone referred to it as a doll they were fined,' remembered Kirk Bozigian, a former product manager at Hasbro, and a catalyst behind the new range of 3¾-inch figures. Bozigian went on to be especially influential in the development of the animated television series *G.I. Joe: A Real American Hero*, and *G.I. Joe: The Movie*, which followed it in 1987.

Dubbed a 'man of action' or 'action figure', Hasbro chief executive Merrill Hassenfeld was convinced that GI Joe held enormous promise, and was confident it would deliver as much for his company as Mr Potato

Head had done previously for so long. Consequently, Hasbro decided to introduce GI Joe in one of the most ambitious launches in toy history.

Protecting the Copyright

To ensure its success however, certain steps had to be taken to prevent competitors copying GI Joe – especially those 'knock-off' merchants likely to rush a cheap clone to market in an unscrupulous attempt to ride on the back of Hasbro's considerable financial investment.

Since the human figure cannot be copyrighted, Hasbro's designers came up with a couple of ingenious ways of protecting their latest venture. Despite having standard and obvious trademark stamps applied discreetly to GI Joe's right buttock, they also applied a distinctive scar to the warrior's right cheek. I'm sure many purchasers of GI Joe assumed this blemish was solely applied to make the little hero look tough and manly. On the contrary, this feature was applied to provide proof of any counterfeiting if it appeared in the same location on a similar figure. Another unique mark of validation, allegedly the unintentional result of a mistake at the pattern-making stage, was the mysterious upside-down thumbnail on GI Joe's right hand.

GI Joe's Launch

Just prior to GI Joe's launch, word inevitably leaked out that Hasbro was up to something, and many in the US toy industry knew that the firm was investing heavily in product development. But for what? When it was finally revealed that all the secrecy concerned a doll for boys, for that is precisely what GI Joe was, reactions were predictably mixed. Despite FW Woolworth being an early supporter, many retail chains believed Hasbro's investment would come to nothing and was doomed to failure – even Stephen Hassenfeld famously said, 'Our decision to market this item was a move based on guts alone.'

The naysayers needn't have worried, however, for as soon as American youth saw the television advertisements for this exciting new toy and began to repeat the catchy lyrics sung to the tune of George Cohen's famous patriotic World War I song 'Over There', they were hooked. In no time American living rooms resounded to the refrain of 'GI Joe, GI Joe, fighting man from head to toe! On the land, on the sea, in the air!'

Hasbro never looked back.

GI Joe a Resounding Success

In its first year the GI Joe range made its debut with an impressive seventy-five different products in the line, each very reasonably priced, with most costing

US toy giant Louis Marx's answer to GI Joe was 'Stony' – 'Stonewall Smith, The Battling Soldier'. Complete boxed versions of this toy are very hard to find in Europe.

'Fighting Yank' was Mego's response to GI Joe.

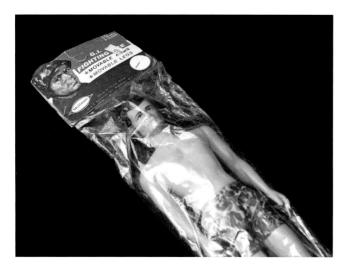

'Fighting Ace' wasn't as neatly packaged as GI Joe. Later, Shillman would produce the 'War Heroes' series of 7-inch fully articulated action figures.

Neither was Shillman's 'Fighting Ace' as neatly articulated as GI Joe.

between $1 and $5; it netted Hasbro sales of a remarkable $23 million. Six million basic figures alone were snapped up within the first twelve months – and this was only the start.

When the initial range of four figures – 'GI Joe Action Soldier', 'Action Marine', 'Action Sailor' and 'Action Pilot' were launched in 1964, Barbie's boyfriend Ken, whom Mattel had launched in 1961, was the only adult male toy figure available on the market. So even sisters had something new to play with, often pinching their brothers' GI Joe and pairing him with Barbie instead of the .50-calibre machine gun he was more suited to. What's more, although Ken had a wardrobe that was almost as extensive as his beau, he didn't have flexible joints and certainly couldn't be positioned in the variety of poses the articulated GI Joe could. GI Joe could get down on his knees and propose to Barbie, but Ken couldn't, so he was no match for GI Joe.

Suddenly, of course, everyone in the US toy business realized they had missed a trick, and that an adult-themed toy figure that pressed all the same buttons for boys as Barbie had with girls, had no opposition. In no time at all, Hasbro's competitors rushed GI Joe copies to market. Some were different enough to avoid litigation, some were downright facsimiles. Mego's 'Fighting Yank' was a toy so similar to GI Joe that Hasbro was able to show that the toy's body had been copied directly from authentic GI Joe tooling; after they threatened a lawsuit, Mego quickly discontinued the product. Mego's 'Fighting Yank' is consequently a real prize amongst collectors today.

Whilst their competitors scrambled to claw a piece of the previously unanticipated market for themselves, rushing out GI Joe copies left, right and centre, Hasbro, the originators, set about supplementing their new action figure with an extensive range of outfits and accessories. Their lawyers could go after the copyists.

TOP: Marx's 'Fighting GI Stony Smith' came with an extensive range of military equipment. '"Stony Smith" has been issued with everything he needs to perform his duties as a fighting GI!', the leaflet claimed. 'Follow the directions for assembling the equipment, then have fun fitting "Stony" with his various outfits.' War needn't be hell.

BOTTOM: Packaging header for Shillman's GI Fighting Ace figure, one of the many toys that jumped on the action figure bandwagon after Hasbro had already laid down the tracks with GI Joe.

STONY (STONEWALL) SMITH

THE FIGHTING G. I. by MARX

Stony Smith has been issued the equipment listed—everything he needs to perform his duties as a fighting G. I.! Follow the directions for assembling the equipment, then have fun fitting Stony with his various outfits.

HEAD TURNS TO RIGHT & LEFT.

SHOULDER FLEXES IN AND OUT— BACK & FORTH

ELBOW BENDS BACK & FORTH

WRIST TURNS ALL AROUND.

AUTHENTIC MILITARY EQUIPMENT

A COLLECTION OF AUTHENTIC MILITARY EQUIPMENT HAS BEEN CAREFULLY SCALED FOR STONY, AND INCLUDES:

HELMET WITH CHIN STRAP
FATIGUE HAT
SPECIAL FORCES BERET
MESS KIT WITH KNIFE, FORK & SPOON
"K" RATIONS
CANTEEN
CANTEEN COVER
CARTRIDGE BELT WITH SCABBARD & BAYONET
CARTRIDGE BELT WITH HOLSTER & G. I. .45
ENTRENCHING TOOL
ENTRENCHING TOOL COVER
HELMET WITH CAMOUFLAGE NETTING AND CHIN STRAP WITH PAD

COMMANDO KNIFE WITH LEG SHEATH ·
M-3 SUBMACHINE GUN
GRENADES
30 CAL. MACHINE GUN
FIELD PACK WITH STRAPS
FIELD GLASSES WITH CASE & STRAPS
WALKIE-TALKIE WITH STRAP
BUGLE
CARBINE WITH SLING
M-1 RIFLE WITH SLING
BROWNING AUTOMATIC RIFLE WITH BIPOD & SLING

HEADGEAR

HELMET WITH CHIN STRAP

ATTACH CHIN STRAP TO HELMET BY PUSHING ENDS OF STRAP THROUGH SLOTS IN HELMET.

SPECIAL FORCES BERET

FATIGUE HAT

K   K

RATIONS

MESS KIT

SLIP END OF BELT THROUGH BUCKLE OF CANTEEN COVER

SNAP COLLAR OVER NECK OF CANTEEN.

FOLD COVER FLAPS OVER CANTEEN & SECURE ON PINS.

CANTEEN

CANTEEN COVER

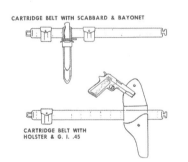

CARTRIDGE BELT WITH SCABBARD & BAYONET

CARTRIDGE BELT WITH HOLSTER & G. I. .45

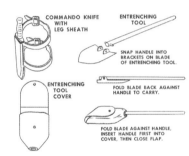

COMMANDO KNIFE WITH LEG SHEATH

ENTRENCHING TOOL

SNAP HANDLE INTO BRACKETS ON BLADE OF ENTRENCHING TOOL.

ENTRENCHING TOOL COVER

FOLD BLADE BACK AGAINST HANDLE TO CARRY.

FOLD BLADE AGAINST HANDLE, INSERT HANDLE FIRST INTO COVER, THEN CLOSE FLAP.

GI Joe Outfits, Equipment and Accessories

From the start, the three figures representing each of the major arms of the military – soldier, sailor and airman – could be outfitted in the widest range of ensembles imaginable. Individual figures were sold boxed and came with only the most basic accoutrements; they were often garbed in fatigues or service overalls, and certainly not in the fashion depicted on the box sides. To achieve a 'ready for battle' appearance it was essential to purchase an accessory set – either one of the more expensive outfit/weapon combinations that came framed in an elaborately engineered

FOR 5 YEARS & OLDER

G.I. FIGHTING ACE
★ MOVABLE ARMS
★ MOVABLE LEGS

$225

Shillman

Made in Hong Kong

GI Joe Japanese World War II infantryman. Now a very rare and collectable figure.

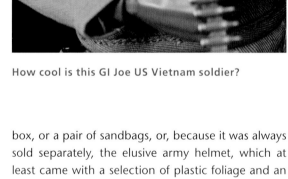

How cool is this GI Joe US Vietnam soldier?

cardboard presentation pack, or one of the cheaper, carded accessory sets that contained individual items such as helmets, field equipment or weapons.

For the Soldier

For soldiers, one of the larger sets might be, for example, a 'Combat Field Jacket Set', which came complete with camouflage jacket, M1 rifle, belted ammo pouches and an assortment of hand grenades (but no helmet). Alternatively, it might be the more elaborate 'Ski Patrol', complete with hooded white one-piece ski suit, a pair of skis, ski poles, Arctic boots and goggles.

Less expensive carded accessory packs offered perhaps a .50-calibre machine gun, tripod and ammo box, or a pair of sandbags, or, because it was always sold separately, the elusive army helmet, which at least came with a selection of plastic foliage and an elasticated loop with which to secure it.

For the Airman

To get the pilot to look anything like the representation on the box containing the figure – you can imagine the disappointment of youngsters who tore open the packaging to discover that the box revealed a figure clad in bright orange overalls, a blue peaked fatigue cap on his head – those who wanted a fully equipped pilot in flight gear had no option but to supplement the basic figure with a number of carded accessory packs. In fact, at least three would be needed, each

Carded 'GI Joe Battle Gear Vietnam Soldier' set produced in 1999 to commemorate his thirty-fifth birthday.

'GI Joe Classic Collection General Colin L. Powell' figure (1998).

of which contained essential items such as the pilot's flying helmet, life jacket or parachute. The flying man could be even further equipped – other accessory sets included a radio pack and his personal side arms.

For the Sailor

The sailor figure at least came more or less ready for action – well, non-violent action aboard ship, that is. The basic sailor was dressed in blue bell-bottoms, black boots, a denim shirt and sailor's cap. But right from the start, the sailor could be upcycled and dressed as a frogman, or even a deep-sea diver in brass helmet and lead boots. However – and there was a pattern here – such enhancement either required the purchase of one of the elaborate and more expensive carded sets, or the acquisition of several acces-

What greeted you when you opened the impressive box of the 'Colin Powell' figure.

sory packs, each of which might contain his rubber jacket and headpiece, another his trousers, another his flippers, and then a final one containing his aqualung cylinders. The deep-sea diver was a substantial outlay, an all-or-nothing acquisition of the complete outfit and ancillary equipment.

All the above reveals the secret to GI Joe's success, and the fulfilment of Hasbro's original objective of creating a product that by its very nature obliged owners to make repeat purchases in order to enjoy the toy to its full potential. Just like the purchasers of Barbie had to do.

For Storage

Youngsters could never have enough uniforms, weapons and other accessories, and very soon enormous stores of arms and equipment could be amassed.

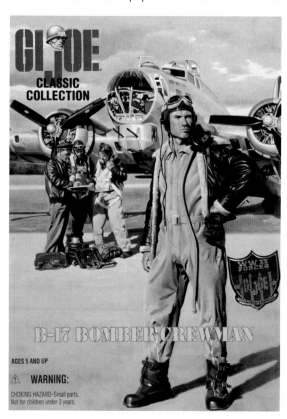

Limited edition 'B-17 Bomber Crewman' produced in the USA by Hasbro in 1997.

Fortunately, GI Joe's manufacturer had thought about the issue of storage for such burgeoning accumulations – they offered a robust wooden foot locker that came complete with a neat vacuum-formed tray in which smaller items could be contained, such as pistols, knives, regalia (even though they were garbed in combat gear, many soldiers' uniforms came complete with medals), maps and map cases and binoculars.

It is an irrefutable fact that today, the kind of action figures we take for granted owe their genesis to an idea mostly pioneered by Stan Weston. They are now as intrinsic to the world of modern toys as yoyos, bats and balls and dolls' houses ever were to previous generations.

We'd nearly given up on 12-inch action figures until Hong Kong's Dragon Models Limited (DML) commenced their fantastic range of 'New Generation Life Action Figure' series in 1999. German 'Grenadier Wilhelm' was one of the first.

'WE CHOOSE TO GO TO THE MOON': ACTION FIGURES IN SPACE

Delivered to a large audience at Rice Stadium in Houston, Texas, on 12 September 1962, President John F. Kennedy's famous speech was the starting gun for the race to the moon. 'We choose to go to the moon in this decade and do the other things,' he said, 'not because they are easy, but because they are hard.' This was not the first time Kennedy had set such a deadline – the previous year he had already informed Congress of his ambitions and invited them to fund a shot at the Moon.

Space Travel

Although NASA did indeed get to the moon before the end of the decade, safely depositing Neil Armstrong and Buzz Aldrin on the lunar surface on 20 July 1969, it was, as Kennedy predicted, a long, hard road and had proved phenomenally expensive to achieve. Participating in the space race, or at least on its periphery, was a much easier contest for US toy manufacturers, and all of them eagerly embraced

Naturally, GI Joe wasn't going to be left rooted to *terra firma*, and in 1966 Hasbro furnished him with a space suit and a Mercury capsule.

It shouldn't be forgotten that up until the United States' moon landing, the USSR consistently scored all the firsts in the space race. Generally unavailable in the West before the collapse of the Soviet Union, these celluloid cosmonaut figures, especially the more elaborate articulated examples, are now becoming increasingly collectable.

the zeitgeist and shot for the stars, many of them successfully launching space missions long before Apollo 11's Eagle lander was anywhere near lift-off, let alone ready for touchdown.

But of course, space travel wasn't a solely American experience – the Soviet Union had stolen a considerable lead in space exploration, securing a succession of early wins and forever holding top place in the record books. The USSR launched Sputnik 1, the first man-made satellite to orbit the earth, on 4 October

1957 and put a dog, Laika, into space a month later, even sending a probe to the moon in 1959 and being the first nation to photograph the dark side of the Earth's only natural satellite soon after. All this, years before their US rivals.

On 12 April 1961, the Soviets crowned all these achievements when cosmonaut Yuri Gagarin circled the Earth in a Vostok spacecraft. They followed this with another win in June 1963, when Valentina Tereshkova became the first woman in space. But, with the Cold War at its bitterest – the Cuban missile crisis took place in October 1962 – in the West attention was firmly focused on how the USA was catching up.

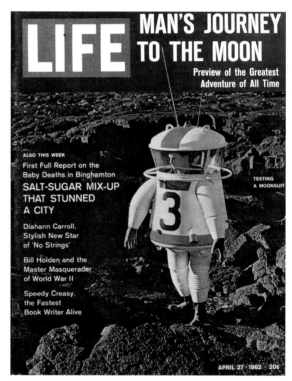

This *Life* cover dates from April 1962 and was inspired by President John F. Kennedy's address to Congress the previous May, when, in response to the Soviet Union's dramatic achievements in space, he announced his goal of sending a man to the moon by the end of the decade, and asked Congress to allocate the funds to pay for it. Inventor Allyn Hazard's iconic moon suit was the inspiration for one of the most popular accessories for Mattel's man in space, 'Major Matt Mason'.

Space Toys

Following Alan Shepherd's brief foray into space in May 1961, toy manufacturers in the West seemed to apotheosize only NASA and its achievements. Nevertheless, children on the eastern side of the iron curtain weren't ignored, and Soviet manufacturers provided them with a variety of patriotic toys of spaceships, Lunokhod moon rovers and plastic spacemen. Unavailable in the West before the collapse of the Soviet Union, many of these figures, especially the colourful articulated celluloid cosmonauts of the early 1960s, now command a premium price amongst collectors.

However, in terms of their numbers and international influence, and their legacy amongst action-figure collectors today, there is no doubt that notwithstanding the slow start of their own nation's space programme, US space toys have long reigned supreme. Ironically, despite the USA initially being on the back foot and playing catch-up with the USSR in the early years, today youngsters might be forgiven for thinking that space exploration is a largely US achievement – a lot of this is down to the fact that most space toys depict only American technology.

MOON SUIT PAK
Adapted from U.S. Space program. You control flexible arm joints. Hammer, screw driver, wrench, radiation detector, too.   #6301
Also available: #6303 Major Matt Mason with MOON SUIT.

'You control flexible arm joints. Hammer, screwdriver, radiation detector, too.' So claimed the leaflet accompanying this fantastic toy.

In 1966, three years before Man set foot on the lunar surface, Mattel introduced their legendary 'Matt Mason' action figure, kitting him out with a faithful replica of Mr Hazard's moon suit.

Hasbro's New Line

In 1966, just two years after the action figure's debut, GI Joe donned a pressure suit and blasted off into space. From now on, US boys were able to outfit him in an authentic silver space suit manufactured from fabric laminated with shiny foil. They could also pop a neat little space helmet on to his head, snapping its movable visor open and shut at will. To complete this out-of-the world package, there was even a high-quality replica of a NASA Mercury space capsule. Combined, astronaut and spacecraft were marketed as being part of the 'GI Joe air force'.

'Action Man's on the launching pad! He's got a helmet, spacesuit, and a whole lot more – and it's all authentically modelled on those used by real live astronauts for Mercury flights,' boasted the sales literature for Hasbro's UK subsidiary Palitoy's astronaut set, which first appeared in 1967.

Hasbro spent a fortune promoting their new line. The television campaign for the range opened with footage showing two young boys playing outside. One of them suddenly chucks his capsule, complete with hapless occupant strapped inside, into a water-filled paddling pool where it lands with a resounding splash. The ad's voice-over was equally ebullient, and a manly voice boomed:

Now a new world of fun with GI Joe air force. Is your GI Joe ready for duty on a carrier? Is he ready to go into space with the new GI Joe astronaut capsule and space suit? Silver uniform, space helmet, communications cord. The realistic capsule has simulated retro rockets, sliding canopy, control panel too. And the capsule floats, so recoveries can be made! There's even a phonograph record of an actual flight. GI Joe is the Greatest. Nothing else is GI Joe!

The GI Joe astronaut came equipped with everything. It was, however, almost impossible to put his foil-coated gloves on his hand without pushing his thumb through the fabric!

The commercial ended with a youngster joyfully exclaiming, 'Boy oh boy, it's a Hasbro toy!'

By the time GI Joe's space capsule was launched in 1966, NASA was coming to the end of its two-man Project Gemini programme and about to focus on the Saturn-powered Apollo moon landings. Nevertheless Hasbro modelled their capsule on the even earlier Project *Mercury* designs for a one-man capsule. Project *Mercury* ran from 1959 through to 1963 with the object of putting a man into Earth orbit and returning him safely back home shortly thereafter, with the USA ideally beating their Soviet rivals to this lofty objective. As we know, the USSR got there first, and Yuri Alekseyevich Gagarin took the laurels on 12 April 1961.

At least purchasers of the GI Joe capsule could console themselves with the fact that although their spaceship wasn't state-of-the-art, it did at least require only one occupant, meaning the purchase of just a single astronaut outfit. As its name suggests, the Gemini capsule that followed Project *Mercury* carried two astronauts, and although they didn't have to be twins, they certainly possessed the right stuff. The Apollo capsule that followed and returned the men from the moon would have been an even more onerous proposition financially, requiring the purchase of three figures.

Hasbro maxed out the excitement and user experience of each capsule purchase by including a 45rpm record in every box. It featured a soundtrack recording of the first American space flight, and was the ideal accompaniment to every youngster's space shot. When the space capsule for Britain's Action Man arrived in 1968 it was identical in every way, but unfortunately came without the 45rpm record, making this disc something of a rarity in the United Kingdom.

'Mattel's Man in Space'

Hasbro's great rival Mattel, whose Barbie had ironically been the trigger for the success of GI Joe in

Moulded in 'Plastizol' over a wire armature, the 'Matt Mason' range included the eponymous hero clad in a white suit, 'Sgt Storm' in a red outfit, astronaut 'Doug Davis' in yellow, and African-American 'Lt Jeff Long' wearing a blue spacesuit.

the first place, were naturally also keen to get in on the space action, and in 1966 they introduced their 'Major Matt Mason' toy line. 'Mattel's Man in Space' was an astronaut who lived and worked on the moon. Interestingly, these figures were initially based on designs publicized in *Life* magazine, most famously on NASA's early concepts for a pressurized moon suit, a version of which Mattel faithfully replicated, and which, curiously, Hasbro ignored.

Matt and his four astronaut colleagues – blond-haired Sgt Storm, who wore a red space suit, civilian astronaut Doug Davis (brown hair and yellow suit) and African American Lt Jeff Long (blue suit) – were moulded from a rubber-like composition called 'Plastizol'. This pliable material, which Mattel also used in their 'Thing Maker' toy line and for their 'Mister Twister' fishing bait, concealed a wire armature,

'Matt Mason' was even furnished with a space station, now a real rarity.

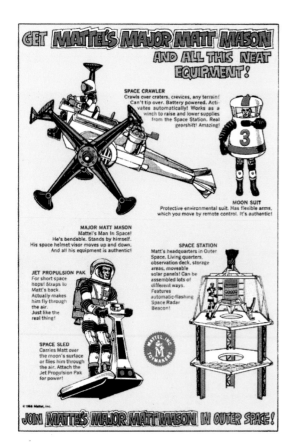

Fans were encouraged to join 'Matt' in outer space and 'get all this neat equipment!'

which permitted the articulation of the astronaut's limbs. Unfortunately this metal skeleton suffered from fatigue, and frequent bending of Matt's arms and legs generally resulted in broken wires, the snapped ends of which would often break through the Plastizol covering, especially at the elbows, knees and hip joints. Consequently, finding original examples of this fifty-year-old plus toy in good condition is becoming more and more difficult.

Whereas Hasbro decided that GI Joe should be based firmly on fact, Mattel went distinctly left field and Matt Mason's world was quickly inhabited by an assortment of space aliens. These included the giant 'Captain Lazer', an ally, and 'Callisto', a Jovian with a transparent green head. 'Scorpio' was a battery-powered insect-like alien, this time with a glowing

Here comes new talking 'Major Matt', his new voice pack strapped to his back. 'Stand by for further instructions', he beams to 'Doug Davis' as he prepares to land on the rough moon terrain. Suddenly, a call for help comes from a distant moon-base...

The 'Major Matt Mason' flight pack came complete with a neat space sled and jet propulsion pack.

head. Matt and the extra-terrestrials enjoyed a wide range of accessories. A three-storey space station was one of the largest in the range, but there was also an array of battery-powered machines, ray guns and jet packs. There was even a book, *Moon Mission*, written by George S. Elrick and illustrated by Dan Spiegle.

When interest in the space programme tailed off in the early 1970s, Mattel dropped the 'Matt Mason' line, but the tiny astronaut's career wasn't over, because allegedly the toy accompanied several US Space Shuttle missions in the role of 'unofficial crewman', and we know for sure that 'Matt' flew on John Glenn's Shuttle flight in 1998.

A. C. Gilbert's 'Moon McDare'

Whereas Mattel's 'Matt Mason' broke new ground because of its dimunitive size (it was less than half as tall as the established 12-inch action figures such as GI Joe) as well as its 'bendy' but vulnerable construction, another US firm, A. C. Gilbert, stayed on the straight and narrow with their own astronaut action figure: 'Moon McDare'.

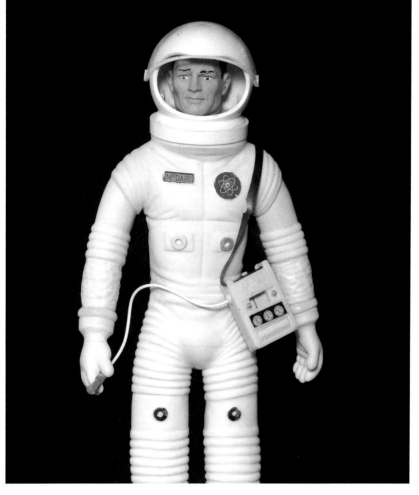

TOP LEFT: **Introduced in 1965, 'Moon McDare' was American company A. C. Gilbert's contribution to the world of astronaut action figures.**

TOP RIGHT: **Boxed 'Moon McDares' came garbed in a smart blue flying suit.**

'Moon McDare' kitted out in all his lunar finery.

Standing 12 inches tall, 'Moon McDare' came as a single figure, clad in a blue flight suit and packed in a striking box. Of traditional construction, Moon McDare was cast in flesh-coloured vinyl but without articulated ball-and-socket joints, and only jointed at the head, shoulders and hips, Gilbert were justifiably proud of their new toy, announcing him thus:

> He's the all-American astronaut, nearly a foot tall and fully jointed for every natural body motion. McDare comes in jump suit and boots, and you can get everything he needs for space walking and moon exploring: a complete, authentic space suit and helmet, oxygen tanks, communications set and many other accessories that really work! His faithful dog, the Space Mutt, comes with his own space suit and equipment.

As with GI Joe, supplementary purchases were necessary to achieve a fully outfitted figure, and there were plenty of accessory packs to be had. First available in

1965 and in the shops until the end of the decade, Moon McDare's accessories included a wide variety of space suits, tools and backpacks. Moon McDare's travelling companion, the canine 'Space Mutt', came complete with its own space suit and helmet!

'Moon McDare' accessory pack, including one of the small air-conditioning units that both cooled and pumped water through the cooling garment worn beneath the space suit.

The battery-operated power pack enabled Moon McDare's blinker light to actually work.

It's debatable what use a spear gun would be in space. The 'Ticking Geiger Counter', however, might be more useful.

Louis Marx Action Figures

New York's Louis Marx & Company naturally got in on the act, too. Already behind a number of successful action figures such as 'Stony Smith', the soldier figure they brought out in 1964 to rival Hasbro's GI Joe, which had been released earlier that year, there was a range of armoured knights and their horses in the 'Noble Knights' series. There was also a really successful assortment of figures based on the adventures of the Lone Ranger and Tonto. Marx's 'Lone Ranger' series was immediately joined by others in what they called their 'Best of the West' range: 'Johnny' and 'Jane West', and youngsters 'Josh' and 'Janice' – any name beginning with 'J' obviously being *de rigueur* at Marx HQ. In 1968 the toy company introduced 'Johnny' and, you guessed it, '*Jane* Apollo', to toy stores.

Moulded in white with flesh-coloured plastic face and hands, and sporting painted brown hair, 'Johnny Apollo' stood only 8 inches tall, occupying the middle ground between Matt Mason and GI Joe in terms of stature. Johnny Apollo's space helmet, back pack and other accessories were moulded in gold, individual items being assembled by the usual snap fixes and interlocking catches; his tubing and piping were fitted with push-fit

TOP: **Moon-landing fervour and Cold-War intrigue during the space race encouraged Louis Marx to introduce their own spaceman, 'Johnny Apollo', in 1968. Like his military predecessor 'Stony', Johnny Apollo was typically well equipped for any imaginable event.**

BOTTOM: **'Johnny Apollo' can be identified by his gold space helmet and white space suit.**

plugs that attached to his space suit and thence into the relevant accessories he either carried or wore. Conversely, Jane Apollo's body was blue, with her hands and head in flesh colour and attachments moulded in white. Her hair was painted a striking golden blonde, her eyes were blue, and her lips were painted a vivid red.

Available boxed as individual figures with limited accessories, Johnny and Jane Apollo could also be purchased in more elaborate gift sets containing either of two space vehicles. With two large spoked wheels capable of negotiating a boulder-strewn lunar landscape, the 'Space Crawler''s cockpit sported an all-encompassing green-tinted transparent canopy. Featuring four wheels this time, each fitted with giant all-terrain tyres, the 'Space Buggy' claimed to be an inter-planet surface vehicle, and appeared to offer better protection for its driver than the 'Space Crawler'. For those extra special occasions, some lucky youngsters might receive the deluxe Lunar Exploration Set, which featured both vehicles and both figures.

Interestingly, children in the UK were granted their own exclusive figure, 'Mark Apollo', who was moulded in white or orange, supported by white accessories.

Eldon's 'Billy Blastoff'

Standing barely 4 inches tall, Eldon's 'Billy Blastoff', a youthful space adventurer with a cheerful face and neat haircut, was clearly aimed at the younger consumer. When he first arrived in 1968, 'Billy' carried two bright red air tanks on his back, which looked more like scuba gear than anything a NASA astronaut might employ. However, following the Apollo land-ings, a year later 'Billy' was remodelled and equipped with a more realistic all-white helmet (his previous one was bright red), and a more businesslike, rectan-gular air-supply back pack, plus a restyled space suit complete with black (as opposed to yellow) gloves.

'Billy Blastoff' was sometimes packaged as a deluxe 'Space Set' with his friend 'Robbie Robot' ('Robbie' was also featured in his own packaged giftset).

'Billy' and 'Robbie' could be purchased separately or parcelled with equipment in a series of action sets.

Another 'Robbie', this time the iconic robot from the 1956 film *Forbidden Planet*, might well have been the inspiration for Ideal Toys' popular 'Zeroids' range, which they introduced in 1967, and from which 'Zerak' is featured here.

Following the momentous achievement of Apollo 11 on 20 July 1969, when Neil Armstrong and Buzz Aldrin stepped on to the moon's surface, there were only five further lunar landings, the last being in December 1972. All told, a total of twelve men have

This is 'Zerak', one of a line of toy robots from the Planet Zero introduced by the Ideal Toy Company in 1967. Science fiction proved almost as popular as science fact – and who knew, until man actually landed on the moon, perhaps Earth's largest satellite *might* harbour mechanical monsters.

walked on the Earth's natural satellite, and for nearly half a century the lunar surface has been spared the tread of human feet.

Other Extra-Terrestrial Achievements

There have, of course, been many other extra-terrestrial achievements since then. Amongst them, highlights include the orbit of the first space station, the USSR's Salyut in 1971, which was followed by the even more ambitious Mir space station, itself in service from 1986 until 2001. Hard on the heels of Soviet developments, the United States' Skylab space station orbited the Earth from 1973 until 1979.

Although beset by fatal design flaws, the Space Shuttle was an enormous achievement and for thirty years until its retirement in 2011, remained at the leading edge of space exploration. Certainly, the International Space Station (ISS), launched in 1998, would *not* have been a feasible objective without it. NASA led the way in extra-vehicular exploration, freeing man from the need to stay inside, or at least connected to a spaceship or station, when in 1984, with the Manned Manoeuvring Unit (MMU) strapped to his back, NASA astronaut Bruce McCandless achieved the first untethered spacewalk.

The World of Sci-Fi

All the above, and other developments, notably the numerous experiments in the various space stations that have been suspended in heavenly orbit, are of course, enormously significant – but to be honest, in the fifty years since the moon landings, space exploration hasn't turned out as many people had expected, especially fans of movies and popular literature. Consequently it has been left to the world of sci-fi to fill the void. Fortunately, several seminal television programmes and films have more than

stepped up to the plate, with the result that they are now the source of some of the best and most collectable action figures for generations.

Two figures, one American and one British, stand head and shoulders above all others as far as influence in the popular sci-fi genre is concerned: Eugene Wesley Rodenberry and Gerry Anderson. Twenty years of age when America entered World War II, Eugene Wesley Rodenberry, better known as Gene, would go on to fly nearly ninety combat missions with the Army Air Force. The coming of peace saw a switch to scriptwriting, and it is for one creation that he will be forever associated: ever since its first broadcast in 1966, *Star Trek* has been the genesis for

The 'Go Bots' were based on figures produced by Popy of Japan (the now-defunct character division of Bandai), named 'Machine Robo'. Toy firm Tonka chose to make the figures sentient robots, rather than human-piloted machines as they had been in Japan.

The 'Transformers: Generation 2' (also known as 'Generation Two' or 'G2') was a Hasbro transformers toy line that ran from 1992–1995.

countless films, television spin-offs, and a bounty of toy collectables.

Gerry Anderson began his career as a trainee with the British Colonial Film Unit, and after an interlude where, like Gene Rodenberry, he too joined the air force, this time during peacetime national service, he resumed his career in the film and television industry. Anderson ultimately established his own company, AP Films, and began a journey in which he created a number of ground-breaking sci-fi series, including classics such as *Stingray*, *Thunderbirds*, *Captain Scarlet* and *Space 1999*. Like *Star Trek*, these and other Anderson properties would yield scores of toy collectables, especially action figures. Zelda, who features on the jacket, is the main villain in Terrahawks, set in the year 2020 when aliens have destroyed NASA's Mars base and now threaten Earth.

Sci-Fi in Japan

Post-World War II, sci-fi gripped the Japanese as strongly as it did Western nations. Subject to the first and thankfully only atomic bombings, Japan was on the receiving end of a scientific nightmare, and it is perhaps no surprise that one of their most successful movies, 1954's *Godzilla*, an allegorical tale of a prehistoric monster awakened by nuclear radiation, gripped the nation's imagination in a particularly apposite manner. Being on the receiving end, nearly, of nuclear Armageddon, encouraged Japanese toy manufacturers and media owners to satisfy an almost endless appetite for sci-fi collectables. At the time

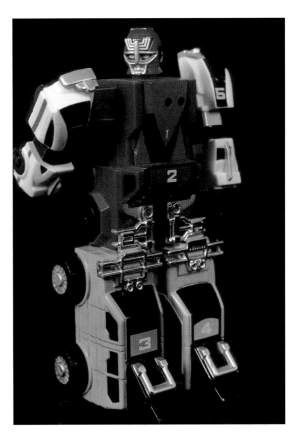

Before Hasbro rebranded them, the first transformer toys were created from two different transforming robot toy lines from Japanese manufacturer Takara, the Car-Robots and Micro Change, from the 'Diaclone' and 'Microman' series' respectively.

Like a Rubik's
Cube, with
a twist here
and there, a
transformer
toy could
change from
one thing, in
this case an
aircraft, into
another, a
mighty robot,
no longer in
disguise.

of writing, more than thirty 'Godzilla' movies have entertained cinema-goers.

Perhaps Godzilla's mutation into an invincible monster encouraged Japanese toymakers to think of other, seemingly benign objects such as motor vehicles and aircraft, which could be *transformed* into unstoppable behemoths. A brief look at some of the major players in this sector makes interesting reading.

Founded in 1955, Japanese toy company Takara's motto, 'Playing is Culture', proved to be particularly apt. As creators of the transforming 'Diaclone' and 'Micro Change' ('Microman') robot series in 1975, Takara was to be the catalyst for a new range of transforming toys, and in 1984 their original toy line was rebranded by Hasbro as transformers. The rest is history.

The most collectable transformers, known as 'Generation One' or 'G1' toys, were available between 1984 and 1992 and featured twenty-eight characters in total – eighteen 'Autobots' and ten 'Decepticons'. The 'Autobots' transform into cars, trucks and even a tractor, whilst the 'Decepticons' change into planes and microcassette recorders, and one changes into a gun.

Under licence to Hasbro, Takara also manufactured and distributed GI Joe toys in Japan. Using the moulds they possessed as part of the licence agreement, Takara also manufactured the 'Henshin Cyborg-1' – a kind of transparent GI Joe with a chrome head and cyborg feet, and whose visible innards revealed an 'atomic engine'.

The oil crisis of the early 1970s resulted in punitive costs for all industries working with plastics, and like so many of its competitors, Takara found it impossible to pass on these price increases to its customers. Figures of a smaller size to the regular 11½-inch ones seemed to offer the only solution if prices were to be kept in check and less plastic used. Consequently, a smaller version of the cyborg toy was developed, standing at only 3¾ inches high. Microman was the result in 1974. The Microman line also introduced the use of interchangeable parts, and laid the foundation for a range of smaller action figures and transforming robot toys.

Gakken, a company founded in Japan in 1946 by

Gakken Henshin 'Robo Legioss' transformer from 1982, one of a growing variety of such toys emanating from Japan.

Hideto Furuoka, principally as a publisher of educational books and toys – and most famous perhaps for their ingenious Denshi Blocks (interchangeable building blocks, each of which contained an electronic component) – also got in on the transforming action-figure act; in fact their Henshin Robo line ('Henshin' means 'transform' in Japanese) from 1982 predates transformers, and surviving mint-in-box examples of these toys are now highly valued by collectors internationally.

Robotech began with an eighty-five episode animé television series, produced by Harmony Gold USA in association with Tatsunoko Production, and first released in the United States in 1985. Action figures were soon available to fans, and originally Matchbox produced these now very rare toys, but later,

AIRFIX

Best known for its plastic construction kits, Airfix was founded by émigré Hungarian businessman Nicolas Kove in London in 1939, and grew to become one of the most famous brands in the world. Indeed, Airfix has almost become a noun, and, regardless of which manufacturer is responsible for the kit being assembled, people often say they are 'doing an Airfix'.

After an amazing eighty years, Airfix is still very much with us, and continues to delight and surprise fans with the quality of its models. However, during its heyday in the 1960s and 70s, Airfix was also a major producer of toys and art and craft materials. Regarding action figures *per se*, it is probably best known for its extensive Airfix 'Eagles' range, but it was also behind a variety of other creations that are now very highly regarded by collectors, and which now achieve top prices at auction. Amongst these were the 'Micronauts', unveiled by the Airfix Products managing director at the 1978 London Toy Fair; the Airfix 'Summer Time Girls' figure range; the short-lived 'Robo-gear' and 'Web Warriors' series (though these were more kits than true action figures, to be honest); and in 1977, of course, their 12-inch 'Farrah Fawcett Majors' doll, produced in association with Mego in the USA.

Interestingly, when I was writing my book *The Other Side of Airfix*, about the company's toys, Jim Dinsdale, a design draughtsman at Airfix in the 1970s, told me about a scheme they had in 1975/76 to work alongside famous pop-culture artist Roger Dean, he of *Yes* and *Osibisa* album-cover fame, to create figures of some of his ideas, such as giant fantastic flies and fantasy creatures, which morphed into dinosaurs. The idea never saw the light of day, but it is interesting to think that Airfix might have been behind the first transforming figures!

Airfix 'Eagles Scuba Diver' (1978).

Airfix licence-built Mego 'Farrah Fawcett Majors' figure (1977).

Boxed and carded
Harmony Gold
Robotech action
figures of 'Lisa
Hayes' and 'Rick
Hunter' (1992).

Harmony Gold themselves provided products in support of the animated series.

Takara's Microman became the basis for the successful 'Micronauts' toy line that Mego sold internationally.

Airfix: A World-Wide Influence

Most famous today for its plastic kits, back in the 1960s and 1970s Airfix also produced a substantial toy range. Some of it was bespoke, created in their South London design offices, but a great deal was produced under licence to American companies such as MPC and Mego. Consequently, Airfix was one of the many international licence holders for 'Micronauts', and examples of their toys have proved very alluring to collectors.

Staying with Airfix whilst working on this manuscript, I had the privilege of talking about action figures to Ralph Ehrmann, the former Chairman of Airfix Industries, and who, most commentators agree, was the financial driving force behind the company in its heyday during the 1960s and 70s.

Airfix released quite a few action figures, including a very collectable 12-inch model of 'Farrah Fawcett-Majors' and the 'Summer Time Girls' – 'with the beautiful hair', a set of three 12.5-inch figures, 'Lazy Days', 'Fun Time' and 'Summer Breeze', as well as their very popular, smaller scale, Airfix 'Eagle' range of figures and action sets designed to appeal to the growing band of fans of the smaller, 3-inch *Star Wars*-type toys.

Interestingly, Ralph told me that he and Airfix managing director John Grey were inspired to produce the 'Eagles' after repeatedly seeing the poor-quality plastic figures that were often inserted as a gift in cereal packets. He recalls:

John and I were both history buffs, and wanted to ensure everything was historically accurate, using the best sculptors available to master the figures. Both John and I were passionate about plastic, and we enjoyed the support of a great team at Airfix. We were all roughly the same age. When we joined Airfix it was in a very unhealthy condition and we fought like hell to improve things, with each new product turning out better than the last.

Ralph knew, and had business dealings with, most of the great names in the toy industry. Of Hasbro's Hassenfeld brothers, he knew Merrill best – his and the American's wives were even involved with the same charitable work.

Ralph also met Louis Marx, and said of him: 'He very much enjoyed his reputation as the "toy king of America".' On one occasion, shortly before leaving for the prestigious and influential Nuremburg Toy Fair, Ralph asked Louis Marx if he would also be attending the show. 'Yes,' Marx answered, 'I'll be there – it's my development department!'

Recalling the heyday of the organization that he built into one of the largest toy companies in the world, in an earlier interview with Juliana Vandegrift of the Victoria and Albert Museum of Childhood in June 2012, Ralph Ehrmann mused about the high price of toys and models today. In the 1960s and 1970s Airfix products – construction kits, toys and arts and craft products – were eminently affordable. He recalls:

> I always believed that you should make things as cheap as possible. Our little soldiers, the ones I told you about which I'm so proud of, they were called 'Hoover Armies' because children used them and scattered them all around the carpet or lino or whatever, and their mothers would have to clean them up. And it didn't matter because they'd get about thirty little soldiers for two shillings.

Action Figures Based on Sci-Fi Movies

Androids and other transformable robots aside, as the twentieth century ended, there were plenty of sci-fi properties that spawned action figures.

1982's movie *Tron* was ahead of the game and predicted many of the developments in computer science that we take for granted today. In the movie, star Jeff Bridges is a computer programmer who is transported inside the software world of a mainframe

In an attempt to capitalize on the craze for smaller figures initiated by those associated with *Star Wars*, in 1978 Airfix introduced their 'Eagles' action figures. This selection features three sets: 'Jaws of the Jungle', 'Mystery of the Pharaohs' and 'Terror of the Deep'.

computer where he interacts with its programs in his effort to escape. In a change from their usual products, Japanese toy company Tomy, who had acquired the toy licence from Disney in 1981, released a hugely successful series of action figures, all of which, especially those in unopened packaging, are now extremely rare.

The 1995 *Apollo 13* movie was directed by Ron Howard and starred Tom Hanks, Kevin Bacon, Bill Paxton, Gary Sinise and Ed Harris. Kenner produced this splendid action figure in association with the docudrama.

The science fiction action-adventure film *Tron* was released in 1982 and was one of the first feature films to use computer animation extensively. Tomy of Japan were granted the licence to produce the official toys of the film, and this is one of their early figures, complete with the very easy to lose 'Disc'.

Amongst others, Mattel released a varied range of figures tied in with *Battlestar Galactica*, the American science-fiction media franchise created by Glen A. Larson, which began in 1978 and told of the conflict between a recently migrated human civilization and a cybernetic race known as the Cylons, bent on their extermination.

Walt Disney Productions' *The Black Hole* premiered the following year and tells the story of the USS *Palomino*, a spacecraft on its way back to Earth, when it and its crew, including the diminutive robot V.I.N.CENT (Vital Information Necessary Centralized), encounter

KENNER

Named after the street in Cincinnati where their original offices were located, Kenner was founded in 1947 by brothers Albert, Phillip and Joseph L. Steiner. A pioneer in the use of television as a medium for advertising toys across the United States, Kenner's early successes included best-sellers such as 'Bubble-Matic', a toy gun that blew bubbles, the 'Girder and Panel' construction toy, the 'Give-a-Show' projector, the 'Easy-Bake Oven', and from 1966 after acquiring it from Denys Fisher, the famous 'Spirograph' drawing toy.

Surrounded by the Kenner Products logo, from the early 1960s the Kenner 'Gooney Bird', the mascot of the company, appeared on most products. It survived until 1974, but the company slogan 'It's Kenner – It's Fun!' endured longer because it was ideal for television.

In 1967 Kenner was purchased by General Mills, who in 1970 merged it with its Rainbow Crafts division to create Kenner Products. This brought the famous Play-

Mint-in-Box Kenner 'Archer' figure from *Small Soldiers* (1998).

Doh modelling compound under the Kenner banner. Amongst toy collectors, however, Kenner Products is most famous for its *Star Wars* action figures and playsets, having acquired the licence for these after Mego rejected it in 1976. Kenner popularized the 3.5-inch action figures – the traditional 12-inch action-figure format making any associated *Star Wars* vehicles and spaceships unfeasible – and between 1976 and 1985 they came to dominate the toy market with these mini marvels. Kenner also produced toys tied in with the 1970s television series *The Six Million Dollar Man*, and enjoyed success with 1979's movie *Alien*.

The 1980s saw the release of the 'Fashion Star Fillies' line of model horses; however, this product was discon-

Kenner 'Robo Cop' figure (1989).

Kenner 'Robin Hood Prince of Thieves Azeem' action figure (1991).

tinued by the end of the decade. But Kenner's 'Super Powers Collection', based on DC Comics superheroes and produced from 1984 to 1986, was enormously successful, the character sculpts based on the actual brand guidelines produced by the originators. Because of its efforts to make the Super Powers Collection as accurate as ever, in 1985 DC Comics named Kenner as one of the honourees in the company's fiftieth anniversary publication, *Fifty Who Made DC Great*.

In the 1980s Kenner also did good business with its *The Real Ghostbusters* figures. These were based on the 1986 to 1991 animated series adaptation of the 1984 movie. Equally popular was its 'Dark Knight Collection', the first of numerous lines based on Batman, launched in 1990.

Kenner Parker was acquired by Tonka in 1987, and both were in turn purchased by Hasbro in 1991. Hasbro closed Kenner's Cincinnati offices in 2000.

In 2010, Hasbro launched 'Star Wars: The Vintage Collection', a series reminiscent of the original Kenner 1978–1984 *Star Wars* line, and in fact branded Kenner. At the time of writing, despite Hasbro scheduling a 2016 release of action figures to support December 2015's release of *Star Wars Episode VII: The Force Awakens*, it appears that a first wave of twelve figures actually hit the shops in advance of the movie's release.

Kenner 'Water World' action figures (1995).

a black hole in space with a large spaceship nearby, somehow defying the hole's massive gravitational pull. Mego were the winners of the franchise war for this production, releasing a wide selection of small, carded figures and more elaborate boxed figures, especially of the inimitable V.I.N.CENT.

Directed by Ron Howard, 1995's *Apollo 13* tells the story of the remarkable achievement of the crew of a moon shot that went badly wrong when a routine procedure accidentally caused a huge explosion in one of the vessel's liquid oxygen tanks. Only by the stoic calmness and professionalism of the Apollo 13's crew, who contrive a repair using bits and pieces of available components, did the mission return home safely. Kenner supported the movie's release with a stunning 12-inch action figure of one of the astronauts, which has since become a very hot collectable indeed.

More than thirty years since the first *Star Wars* movie premiered, in 1999 George Lucas's *Star Wars: Episode I – The Phantom Menace* became the first instalment in the prequel trilogy that continued with 2002's *Star Wars: Episode II – Attack of the Clones* and 2005's *Star Wars: Episode III – Revenge of the Sith*. Inevitably, all these movies generated a huge output of licensed toys, most of them action figures produced by Hasbro.

Many films such as *Alien*, its sequel *Aliens* and the subsequent franchise, weren't supported by much in the way of action figures when first released in the 1980s. In fact it wasn't until 1992 that Kenner's *Aliens* toys appeared, and they were originally intended to support a children's animated series, *Operation: Aliens*, which didn't materialize, rather than the previous movies. In 1998 Kenner followed these figures with a new line, 'Aliens: Hive Wars', which for some reason included 'Predator' figures as well.

The twenty-first century has seen dozens of action-figure series based on much earlier sci-fi movies, especially those in the *Alien* and *Predator* franchises. Manufacturers such as NECA and McFarlane Toys have led the way in this field.

James Cameron wrote, produced, directed, and even co-edited 2009's smash hit *Avatar*, about the mid-twenty-second-century human colonization of the planet Pandora and the mining of the mineral unobtainium located on it. Cameron intended to commence work on *Avatar* immediately following his 1997 blockbuster *Titanic*, but his vision was too far ahead of the digital technology available at the time. When it was released, *Avatar* became the highest grossing film of all time, knocking the incumbent, his other movie, *Titanic*, off the top spot, which it had held for twelve years.

Mattel secured the action-figure licence for *Avatar* in 2009, releasing figures of the main protagonists, Jake Sully and Dr Grace Augustine, in both their mortal and avatar incarnations (Sully was also available in his finely detailed wheelchair). The unsympathetic Colonel Miles Quaritch and his troops were also produced, the range reaching its high point with accurate representations of the Omaticaya clan, notably the 'star' of the movie Neytiri, the hunter Tsu'Tey, and the six-legged Direhorse.

NECA REEL TOYS

America's New Jersey-based National Entertainment Collectables Association, or NECA, specializes in producing action figures typically licensed from films, videogames, sports, music and television series. The company was founded in 1996, and now has over sixty licences for which it produces products. These include *A Nightmare on Elm Street*, *Alien*, *Batman*, *Pacific Rim*, *Guardians of the Galaxy*, *Planet of the Apes*, *Predator*, *Robocop*, *Rambo*, *Rocky*, *Scream*, *Divergent*, *Shaun of the Dead*, *Assassin's Creed*, *The Avengers*, *The Hunger Games*, *Halo* and a wide range of other Marvel and *Musters of the Universe* figures.

NECA's Reel Toys division was formed in 2002 expressly to cater for the demands of action figure and toy enthusiasts and released collectables, rather than toys, and consequently was able to acquire properties that other manufacturers (other than McFarlane Toys perhaps) would consider unsuitable for children and tyros.

VIVID IMAGINATIONS

Vivid Imaginations was founded in 1992 by former Matchbox UK managing director Nick Austin and finance director Alan Bennie. Based in Guildford, Surrey, Vivid manufactures, designs and distributes toys, and holds the distribution rights on a number of television shows and films. 'Captain Scarlet' was the first of many distribution deals, and over the years Vivid has produced toys for *Thunderbirds*, *The Simpsons*, *Cars*, *Shrek*, *Toy Story 3*, WWE, Disney, and Bratz. Vivid has also produced dolls based on Take That, JLS, The Wanted, One Direction and Justin Bieber.

The leading Independent Toys and Games Group in Europe, Vivid also has offices in Paris, Frankfurt and Hong Kong. The company's two founders were recently awarded Lifetime Achievement Awards by the British Toy & Hobby Association.

In 1997, when Hasbro ceased production of Sindy, the doll was licensed to Vivid Imaginations.

All of Vivid's in-house products are designed in the UK by British designers, and are made in factories in China.

Vivid Imaginations 'Captain Scarlet' action figure (1993).

Vivid Imaginations 'Space Precinct Police Bike' and figures (1994).

THE RESPONSE TO THE REVOLUTION IN BOYS' TOYS

Inevitably, the runaway success of GI Joe encouraged other toy companies to try and emulate Hasbro's success, and it didn't take long for myriad copycats to hit the shops. Familiar with the strictures protecting intellectual property ownership, and well aware of the measures Hasbro would have taken to protect their new action figure, established companies were careful to steer clear of releasing anything that could have been considered plagiarism. Smaller manufacturers, however, and especially those based in the Far East, were much less circumspect, and throughout the 1960s and on into the early seventies they sailed too close to the wind. GI Joe knockoffs abounded.

After GI Joe was gifted to Palitoy in the UK, Hasbro's dominion over the action figure was made clear on the rear of its lower torso.

The Toy Giants Protect Their Copyright

Even the most brazen imitators appreciated that releasing an action figure with the prefix 'GI' was asking for trouble, but because the term 'action figure' had bedded into the popular consciousness, and Action Man was soon to be an established brand name in the United Kingdom and Europe, *action* was considered fair game.

In addition to Stanley Weston's attempt at emulating the GI Joe concept with his 'Captain Action' for the Ideal Toy Company, there was also 'Johnny Action', 'Johnny Combat', 'Johnnie Goes to War', 'Bruce Action', 'Action Buddy', 'Action Joe', 'Action Jackson', 'Mr Action', 'Combat Man', 'Fighting Ace', 'Fighting Yank' and… the 'Action All Stars'.

Rosko Industries' 'Johnny Hero', which later became 'Olympic Hero', was another contender. GM Toys brought out 'Super Mike', and a Hong Kong manufacturer made a 'Sergeant Mike!' German toy manufacturer, the Simba Dickie Group, produced 'Dickie Action'. In the USA there was 'Action Gary' and 'Action Tina', and France's Gégé produced their own Action Man lookalike complete with scar. And once Britain's Palitoy had picked up the baton and begun to produce GI Joe under licence after rechristening him Action Man, there would even be an 'Action Girl', to compete with the new smaller 3-inch figures mostly associated with *Star Wars: Action Force*.

It was all action.

Manufacturers in the Far East, most notably those

Introduced by Rosko Industries in 1965, 'Johnny Hero' was another large action figure rushed to market after Hasbro's GI Joe revealed that boys were as keen as girls to dress and undress doll-like toys. Later the figure was repackaged as 'Olympic Hero'.

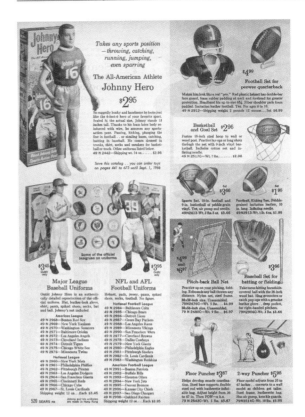

'So ruggedly hunky and handsome he looks, just like the six-foot-six hero of your favorite sport,' boasted this full-page advertisement for 'The All-American Athlete 'Johnny Hero''. 'Passing, kicking, plunging the line in football... or stealing bases, catching, batting in baseball.'

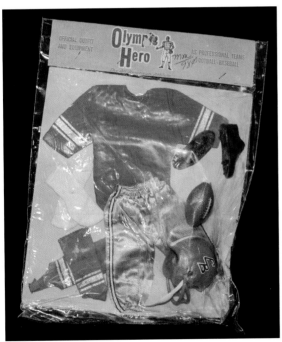

Complete 'Olympic Hero' US football (soccer) outfit. Due to the lack of protection from this very simple packaging, it is uncommon to find the relatively fragile plastic helmet without damage.

in Hong Kong, were far enough away geographically from Hasbro in the USA and their licensee Palitoy in England to feel confident that they could risk 'passing off', as lawyers call copying. Anyway, in the days before high-speed communications, it would take a very long time to track down the real copyists, and even if they were identified, would it be worth the cost of trying to pursue them through the courts?

Hasbro and Palitoy weren't overly concerned because it was obvious that the quality of their offering would be far superior to the figures produced by any unscrupulous imitator, most of whom would have to resort to cheap blow-moulded processes – these produced thin-walled components lacking the articulation and sturdiness of the genuine article, the components of which utilized more costly injection

'Adventure Man' was another GI Joe/Action Man 'me too'. Produced in Hong Kong by the now little-known British company Cecil Coleman, it offered fantastic value for money.

and rotational moulding processes. In addition, the big boys had laced their own products with numerous discreet features, which if copied would quickly reveal the work of counterfeiters. They also employed legions of copyright lawyers.

I first met Keith Melville in the early 1980s when I was writing *The Model World of Airfix*, the first published profile of the famous plastic construction kit manufacturer (and my first book to boot). Back then, Airfix had just been plucked from receivership by US Giant General Mills, who tasked their British subsidiary Palitoy with the management of the company, moving it from its traditional home in south London to Coalville in Leicestershire. Palitoy had become the home to two iconic British brands: Action Man and Airfix.

I had been introduced to Keith and his colleague David Wicks by Peter Allen, the three of them being responsible for the design of Airfix kits at Palitoy. After losing touch for some years, but aware that he was still in contact with some of those who worked on the Action Man line, Keith and I renewed our acquaintance. Keith told me:

We at Airfix all got put over to Action Man in the death throes of Palitoy. What I can remember was that the new items were completely up to date, detail wise and in scale, which interested us, as that is what we were used to at Airfix. I used to think that John Hawkes, who was the Director of Design and Development at Palitoy (previously Product Development Manager at the 'old' Airfix), thought that he was flogging a dead horse, as nobody seemed to be interested – they were all waiting for the axe to fall, which it did. It was a very sad end to a vibrant, intelligent design faculty that produced excellent toys, models and trains.

The Action Force Figures

Keith explained that the demise of Palitoy wasn't the end of the line for him and other Airfix veterans:

Then I moved to Hasbro with Peter (Allen) and got involved with the Action Force figures, includ-

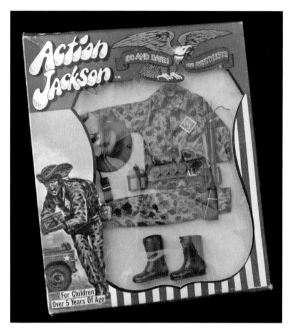

'Action Jackson' was Mego's first foray into the realm of action figures, and established the firm's regular practice of producing action figures with interchangeable bodies. Generic bodies could be reused, and new figures created by interposing different heads and costumes on what was already in the bag.

Australia's commitment to the Vietnam War started with a small body of thirty military advisers in 1962, and increased over the following decade to a peak of 7,672 Australian personnel. Mego's 'Action Jackson' tropical uniform reflected the nation's sacrifice.

ing an absolute scale rendition of an F-14 Tomcat which could carry two figures. It was superb, and of course only the Americans could produce anything like that. The small figures at that time were getting more detailed with lots of accessories, and it was mostly a case of changing packaging and small items to pass UK and European toy laws and safety specs.

After leaving Hasbro Bradley (Hasbro had acquired Milton Bradley in 1984), Keith went to the then Crown Colony of Hong Kong and joined Lanard Toys, a company founded in 1978 that had an established range of pre-school toys, plus an interesting assortment of toy power tools aimed at older children. In 1988 Lanard had launched their very popular 'The CORPS!' range of fully articulated action figures. Currently, Lanard Toys has established an enviable reputation for a wide variety of toys, collectables, arts and crafts materials and outdoor playthings.

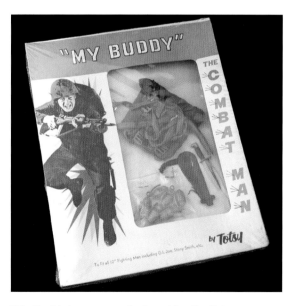

'My Buddy' was manufactured by the Totsy Manufacturing Company from Massachusetts, and designed to fit both GI Joe and Stony Smith.

'Military Buddy' was yet another Hong Kong-produced GI Joe also-ran. It is not to be confused with the Louis Marx 'Canadian Buddy' action figure, which was sold only for a brief period, first appearing in the 1967 Simpsons-Sears Christmas catalogue, and then disappearing altogether.

'I wasn't done with Action Force yet,' said Keith, 'because when I went to live in Hong Kong for a while and worked for Lanard Toys I was involved with their own version of these figures, which you could interchange with the Hasbro versions.'

Keith told me that Hasbro was very protective of its Action Force figures, and every time Lanard, or any of the other competitors who produced figures of the same size, brought something they considered too similar to market, the toy giant always resorted to the threat of legal sanction:

> Hasbro have a full-time legal department who look at every new toy on the market to see if it infringes

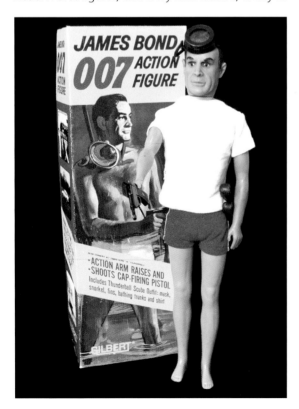

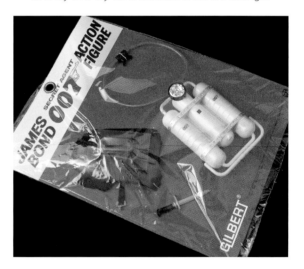

Gilbert's 'James Bond' figures and accessories took advantage both of boys' surprising penchant for playing with doll-like toys, and the phenomenal success of the 007 franchise. It was produced to coincide with the release of *Thunderball* in 1965. 'Action Arm Raises and Shoots Cap-Firing Pistol,' the box boasted. 'Includes Thunderball Scuba Outfit: mask, snorkel fins, bathing trunks and shirt.'

on their territory. If it does, and their own product is fully copyrighted, they will act. They didn't succeed with my old company, Lanard, as the size of the small figures hadn't been copyrighted, so anyone could make them unless they were direct duplicates. Lanard never did that, as all their figures were original. I think that Hasbro took umbrage because all the fixings appeared to be identical. You could take the front body of a Hasbro figure and match it up perfectly with the back of a Lanard figure and use the same screw fixings. The same could be done with the arms and legs. Lanard quite rightly promoted them as a versatile extension to the toy box and a fitting addition to existing figures on the market. 'Use them with other action figures to enhance your fun,' they urged purchasers. Which they certainly did.

Keith remembers proudly that Hasbro figures and accessories were much more lifelike and technically correct than other mini figures on the market: 'I found that at Hasbro when I was given an F-14 Tomcat for two Action Force figures to fit in, it was perfectly in scale. Other small figure companies tended to caricature the figures and accessories, but not Hasbro,' he recollected.

US Giant: Louis Marx and Company

Alongside Hasbro and Mattel, there was really only one other US giant (by now, although Ideal Toys marketed some action figures, most notably an articulated miniature of Evel Knievel, they had mostly diversified into games) and that was Louis Marx and Company.

Marx completed the triumvirate of leading toy companies in America, and after GI Joe's introduction they rushed out a direct competitor, a soldier character known as 'Stony Smith'.

Stony Smith was far less well articulated than Hasbro's figure (he only gained articulated knee joints in 1965, and prior to that only his arms bent),

and possessed just one uniform, which was moulded on in relief, rather than being a removable fabric outfit. To avoid accusations of copycat behaviour, 'Stony' was significantly shorter than GI Joe, being only 8 inches tall as against Joe's height of 12 inches. However, by the late 1960s, realizing that 'Stony' stood little of chance of competing against Hasbro's action figure, not least because their advertising campaigns were no match for what Hasbro was spending on GI Joe (Marx were famous for the frugality of their marketing budget), Louis Marx moved on. Collectors should note that 'Stony' was later repackaged under the names 'All American Fighter' and 'Buddy Charlie'.

He may have lost the battle with GI Joe, but today 'Stony' is a real winner, certainly as far as his financial worth to collectors is concerned. At the time of writing, boxed, complete 'Stony' action figures can command prices in excess of even Hasbro's soldier.

Moving on from military figures, Marx initially attempted to capitalize on the craze for espionage that kept youngsters glued to their television

Designed and manufactured by Barter in Hong Kong, 'Dynaman' was an 'English soldier'. In the 1970s they would also produce the smaller 'Tiny Tuffys' (sic) range.

'Big Jim' was a popular line of action-figure toys produced from 1972 through to 1986 by Mattel for the North American and European markets. Less militaristic than GI Joe, 'Big Jim' leant more towards the world of espionage. 'Professor OBB's character was partially based on James Bond's 'Doctor No'.

screens watching programmes such as *The Man from U.N.C.L.E.*, *Get Smart* and *Mission: Impossible*. 'Mike Hazard Double Agent' was the result. But, like 'Stony', this figure was also short-lived, and consequently, just like 'Stony', it is now very collectable.

Other, more generic historical periods appeared to offer more longevity, and around the time Marx had hoped that the cloak-and-dagger world of espionage might be the answer, they also investigated two periods from yesteryear. Who needs World War II when there's the age of chivalric knights or the gun-slinging days of the Wild West?

A little bruised and battered perhaps, but Louis Marx decided to chart a new course, and as we shall see below, finally discovered that mediaeval Europe and the rough and tough days of the US frontier would provide the results that previous ventures had failed to yield.

Marx Rises to Prominence

But before we investigate figures from the 'Noble Knight' or 'Best of the West' ranges, I think it is worth spending a little time looking at how Marx, one of the outstanding American toy companies, rose to such prominence.

Founder Louis Marx was born in Brooklyn, New York, in 1896. His career in toys began when he was only fifteen, working for Ferdinand Strauss, a manufacturer of mechanical playthings. By the age of twenty, Marx was managing one of Strauss's factories. Marx then entered the United States Army as a private, and attained the rank of sergeant before returning to civilian life in 1918. He loved army life and perpetually remained fascinated with all things military.

In 1919 Louis and his brother David founded their eponymous company. After Strauss's business hit the rocks, the Marx brothers (sic) purchased some of the surviving machine tools from their previous employer, repurposing some of Strauss's bestsellers as Marx-branded products. These proved to be just as successful as they had been in their original incarnations, and soon Marx was also rapidly adding its own archetypes to the company's inventory. At the age of twenty-six, Louis Marx was a millionaire.

Immediately post-World War II, with twelve facto-ries worldwide, the Marx company was the largest toy manufacturer in the world. Employed as a government consultant to advise foreign governments regarding the reconstruction of their toy industries following the devastation of total war, Louis Marx took networking to new levels, making valuable contacts amongst manufacturers in Europe and Japan, territories in which he briskly established manufacturing plant.

DUNBEE-COMBEX-MARX

After Louis Marx retired from the toy business, he sold his company to Quaker Oats in 1976; however, the purchase did not provide the benefits the manufacturer of breakfast cereals had hoped for. Marx had failed to keep up with the evolving revolution in electronic toys that had encouraged other manufacturers to comprehensively adopt components such as transistors and circuitry boards. Another Quaker brand, Fisher-Price, was amongst the early adopters, and willingly embraced new technology, with the effect that Marx's shortcomings were made more manifest.

Another problem with Marx was that even after their founder's departure, their continued predilection towards military toys didn't sit well within a firm founded on pacifistic, anti-war principles. After closing the two major Marx plants in Pennsylvania, in early 1976 Quaker sold its struggling Marx division to the British conglomerate Dunbee-Combex-Marx, so named after they had previously purchased Marx's UK subsidiary in 1967.

Dunbee-Combex had partially evolved from a Yorkshire toy company called Green Monk Combex, which had been founded in Yorkshire in 1946 and had earned an enviable reputation for a variety of kaleidoscopes and robust tinplate toys such as their enormously popular 'Sooty Songster Xylophone'.

Following Lines Brothers' collapse in 1971, Tri-ang Hornby was also acquired by Dunbee-Combex-Marx, becoming Hornby Railways. However, by 1976 Hornby was facing challenges from Palitoy and Airfix, both of whom made model railways of a similar quality, but which, because they were manufactured in Hong Kong, were significantly cheaper. In 1954 Lines Bros moved production of their trains (then called Tri-ang Railways) to a new factory in Margate, Kent, and this soon became Rovex Scale Models Ltd. So incestuous is the British toy industry that the Rovex factory was once the home of the famous FROG plastic construction kits; today it is where its great rival, Airfix, resides. Following Lines Bros disintegration, it acquired Dinky Toys in 1971. And this famous brand had been founded by none other than Frank Hornby of Meccano fame in 1934.

Dunbee-Combex-Marx, or DCM as it rebranded itself, hoped that the acquisition of Marx's American and Hong Kong holdings might provide the opportunity for them to introduce 'Sindy', one of former Lines Bros subsidiary Pedigree's most successful products, which they also owned, to an eager US market. But despite being given a make-over intended to make Sindy more appealing to American girls, and simultaneously pinch business from Mattel, owners of Barbie, the transformation of a British success wasn't enough to lure our trans-Atlantic cousins away from their home-grown product.

Even successful figure ranges based on the BBC's popular *Camberwick Green* television series, which sold well in the UK but nowhere else, could do nothing to reverse DCM's fortunes, and the company began to falter. Like many British toymakers in the late 1970s, DCM suffered from the effects of the general economic downturn. High inflation made home-grown products expensive, and by the end of the decade the company was unable to keep its head above the water, and as a result filed for bankruptcy.

Louis Marx retired in 1972, selling his company to Quaker Oats, who also owned the Fisher-Price toy brand, for $54 million. Unfortunately, the expected benefits between the two toy brands didn't work out as Quaker had hoped, and in early 1976 they sold their Marx division to a British conglomerate, Dunbee-Combex-Marx, who had already acquired the former Marx UK subsidiary in 1967.

Britain's struggling economy in the late 1970s ultimately resulted in the collapse of Dunbee-Combex-Marx. By the early 1980s, many Marx trademarks, patterns and mould tools had been sold off to other toy manufacturers, and to one in particular, Mego Corporation, which was already an established producer of action figures.

Marx Playsets

Before they got into action figures, Marx had gained a great deal of experience with miniature figures. Since the early 1950s Marx Playsets, compendiums of figures, forts and castles, had proved enormously popular and delivered profitable business for the company. Some of the most successful playsets included the 'Roy Rogers Rodeo Ranch', Walt Disney's 'Davy Crockett at the Alamo', 'The Rifleman Ranch', 'Battle of the Blue and Grey', 'The Battle of the Little Big Horn', 'Ben Hur' and 'Fort Apache'. The burgeoning space race encouraged the release of sets such as 'Rex Mars', 'Moon Base' and 'Cape Canaveral'. As the reader might imagine, all of the above command the highest values amongst the collecting fraternity.

Often packed in tinplate carrying cases that unfolded, the sides of the case ingeniously formed part of the structure of whatever building was involved – a castle, or 7th Cavalry fort, for example. These playsets were packed to the brim with figures, buildings and accessories, and all available for a bargain price of between $4 and $7. Even bumper sets such as the giant 'Ben Hur Playset', which came out in time for Christmas 1959 and rode high on the wave of the successful Charlton Heston movie, and which came packed with Romans, gladiators – even a scale coli-

seum – sold for little more than $10. Marx's proud slogan of 'more for less' was never more appropriate.

It wasn't long before Marx began producing separate figures to add to those that came with the playsets. In 1953, the first set of what collectors call the 'First Issue Knights' became available. However, these were relatively small in scale, initially just 54mm in size, the same size as traditional toy soldiers. By the early 1960s these figures had grown to a more substantial height of 6 inches, and sales were prolific.

In 1963, Marx began making the 'Nutty Mads', a series of beatnik-style plastic figurines such as 'Donald the Demon' – a half-duck, half-madman driving a miniature car. In fact these creations were in tune with the zeitgeist of the times, when counterculture characters such as 'Big Daddy Ed Roth', creator of 'Rat Fink' and the inspiration behind the hot road vehicles produced by Revell, or the 'Weird-Oh's' rendered by Hawk Models in the USA and marketed under licence in the UK by Airfix, had become all the rage.

The Noble Knight Series

With so many swashbuckling movies about, especially the 20th Century Fox movie, *Prince Valiant*, knights and mediaeval warriors appeared to be what youngsters wanted most. Beatniks and hippies could wait perhaps, but armoured knights would do for Marx what marines in camouflaged fatigues were doing for Hasbro.

Soon after GI Joe had proved that boys liked to dress and undress dolls – sorry, action figures – just as much as their sisters did, Marx took the plunge and released their fully articulated 'Noble Knights'. These superbly moulded figures came complete with suits of clip-on armour, and could even be mounted on armoured horses. They took the market by storm.

The 'Noble Knight' series first appeared in 1968 and sold until 1973. The knights were manufactured to the same 1:6- (12-inch) scale as GI Joe. 'Sir Gordon' was the Gold Knight, 'Sir Stuart' the Silver Knight, and there was also 'Sir Cedric', the Black Knight, a figure produced at the Marx factory in Swansea, South

Marx's 'Noble Knights' series first appeared in 1968 and was available until 1973. 'Sir Gordon' was the Gold Knight, and in addition there was 'Sir Stuart' the Silver Knight and armoured horses for all of them. In the UK there was also a Black Knight, which is now very rare. Later, a pair of Vikings were added to the range, and these also came with horses.

Wales, and principally targeted at the UK market. Consequently, it is now very rare. The UK editions of the Gold and Silver Knights also had alternative names, 'Sir Percival' and 'Sir Roland' respectively.

Superb armoured horses could be purchased separately as mounts for the knights. The 'Noble Knights' could draw upon a veritable armoury of weaponry, including swords, knives, wheel-lock pistols, crossbows, halberds, flails and maces. There were also a couple of Vikings: 'Eric' and 'Odin', the Viking chieftain, both of whom could also be mounted on appropriate horses.

So popular were the Marx knights that it comes as no surprise that in recent years, other manufacturers have obtained the rights to release replicas of them. First there was a Mexican company, Plastimarx, who in the 1980s released 'Sir Gordon', the Gold Knight. In 1998, a now defunct US toy retailer, K-B Toys, sold

remakes of the Gold and Silver Knights. In 2001, one of the many US companies that had acquired access to Marx mould tools re-released the vintage 'Sir Brandon', the Blue Knight, in new packaging. Vikings 'Odin' and 'Erik' soon followed.

Although they are far from vintage or original, since their release even these contemporary replicas have appreciated in value and are now highly sought after by collectors. One of the reasons is that the originals are over fifty years old, and finding complete, mint-in-box originals today is almost impossible. Another reason for the popularity of such reproductions is that they provide a source for components missing from vintage sets – spare parts – in the same way that Action Man collectors discovered that the 40th anniversary revival sets released by Modellers Loft in 2006 provided a treasure trove of replacement parts from Palitoy's heyday.

Like the Action Man 40th sets, for which Modellers Loft's Alan Hall allegedly sacrificed countless valuable vintage parts and packaging components for use as patterns, moulded from the original tools, Marx reissues were identical to their predecessors.

'Best of the West' Series

As I mentioned above, the other genre Marx made their own was the Wild West, and in the mid-1960s the company established a family of figures, a series titled the 'Best of the West', where the main character was a cowboy named 'Johnny West'.

'Johnny' was soon joined by an Indian named 'Chief Cherokee', who rode a horse named 'Thunderbolt', and in 1966 by a cowgirl 'Jane West' and her range horse 'Flame'. More horses, teepees, a corral and even a jeep and trailer were soon added to the 'Best of the West' range. In 1967, two girls, 'Josie' and 'Janice', and two boys, 'Jay' and 'Jamie', joined the family. The children had a pony, 'Poncho', and two dogs – 'Flick', a German shepherd and 'Flack', an English setter.

The West family lived in a traditional homestead, Circle X Ranch (after the Marx trademark!), which was made of cardboard. For outings, they could ride in a scale replica buckboard, or for longer trips, a covered wagon. The available accessories appeared endless

The 'Fort Apache Fighters Series' was developed as an offshoot of the 'Best of the West' collection, and two additional Indians, 'Geronimo' and 'Fighting Eagle', joined the tribe. In 1968, a 'General Custer'

'Johnny West's son, 'Jay West', was just one of a line of action figures in the 'Best of the West' range marketed by Marx to compete with GI Joe. There were also two girls, 'Josie' and 'Janice', and another son, 'Jamie'. The range also included gambler 'Sam Cobra', native American 'Chief Cherokee', as well as 'Captain Maddox', 'Zeb Zachary', 'Bill Buck' and two additional Indians named 'Geronimo' and 'Fighting Eagle'. Horses, buckboards, tepees, even an Indian princess amongst others, together created a substantial range of figures.

ABOVE: **Louis Marx 'Lone Ranger' figure in its original box from 1973.**

figure was added, as was a full-scale cardboard 'Fort Apache'.

In the early 1970s, Western bad man and gambler 'Sam Cobra' arrived. Fortunately a lawman, 'Sheriff Garrett', was on hand to apprehend Sam if necessary. Marx eventually produced native American royalty with the appearance of 'Princess Wildflower'.

In 1975, after ten years of continuous 'Johnny West' production, Marx changed the name of their Western-themed action figures, and the 'Johnny West Adventure Series' was born. The toy company released 'Quick Draw' versions of 'Johnny West' and 'Sam Cobra': when a lever in the figure's back was

'The Masked Rider hits the trail once more, on Silver his horse, and with Tonto his trusty Indian companion.' This advertisement is typical of those gracing boys' comics and promoting Marx action figures to an eager audience. 'This fully movable cowboy is complete in every detail.'

provenance. As can be imagined, these figures are amongst the most highly valued items for die-hard fans of Louis Marx and Co.'s impressive output.

Where would the 'Lone Ranger' be without his faithful native American companion 'Tonto'?

Reviver of retro toys and construction kits, Playing Mantis resurrected the 'Action Jackson' figure range at the turn of the twenty-first century.

operated, they were able to draw their pistols. Marx also introduced 'Jed Gibson', a black cavalry scout, a figure now highly desired by enthusiasts.

Bringing the story right up to date, in 2015 American toy collector James Wozniak's enterprise, Classic Recasts, was granted permission to produce a limited edition of only 200 50th anniversary 'Johnny West' 1965–2015 figures. These came complete with an excellent repro box, figure and all accessories, and of course, a certificate guaranteeing the figure's

ACTION MAN: GI JOE CROSSES THE POND AND PALITOY MAKES ITS MARK

Background to Palitoy's Toy Division

Palitoy was formerly Alfred Pallet's Cascelloid Ltd, which he founded in 1919; in 1968 it was acquired by US food conglomerate General Mills, and incorporated into the company's toy division CPG (Creative Products Group). Before this, the Leicester-based business had established an enviable reputation as a manufacturer of dolls. The first of these was in 1925: Mabel Lucy Attwell's 'Diddums', which together with being an early example of character licensing, was also one of the first blow-moulded toys (the process involving super-heated steam channelled between two sheets of celluloid in a mould). Like Cascelloid's other products, 'Diddums' was sold in quantity via the high-street retailer FW Woolworth.

Because of Cascelloid's reputation for innovation – they regularly introduced new materials and the manufacturing techniques required to get the most from them – by the late 1930s they had earned the nickname 'The House of Constant Progress'.

In the early 1930s Alfred Pallet bought the exclusive worldwide rights to manufacture products using 'Plastex', a new form of 'unbreakable' plastic that proved more durable than celluloid. In 1935 Bexoid, a non-flammable material, and with it a range of 'Bexoid Cherub' dolls, was introduced. One of these dolls was presented to Queen Mary at the 1935 British Industries Fair, generating a great deal of valuable publicity and interest from the toy trade.

Initially associated with the company's new ranges of soft-bodied dolls produced at the company's new factory in Coalville, Leicestershire, the 'Palitoy Playthings' trademark was introduced in 1937.

During World War II Palitoy's Coalville factory was requisitioned in aid of Britain's war effort. Dolls were put on the backburner in favour of the production of anti-gas eye shields and bomb fins made from laminated paper. However, this did not prevent A. Pallet from registering several patents he thought would come in useful when Cascelloid's normal production resumed. Consequently, ideas for the practical integration of 'sleeping eyes' in vinyl dolls, and concepts for 'Patsy', the first vinyl drinking-wetting-crying doll, were filed ready for the coming of peace.

In 1947, Bill Pugh, a man whose name would forever be linked with Action Man, joined Cascelloid as chief designer.

In the early 1960s, Palitoy, as Cascelloid was by now better known, made a bid for the burgeoning market amongst teenage girls. Manufacturing under licence to their US originators, in 1964 the Leicestershire factory began to manufacture the 'Tressy' doll, and a year later in 1965 launched 'Tiny Tears' to the UK market. The following year, in 1966, Palitoy won the National Association of Toy Retailers' Girls' Toy of the Year Award. That year, the toy division at Coalville was

PALITOY

Alfred Edward Pallett founded The Cascelloid Company in Coalville, Leicestershire, in 1919. As its name suggests, Pallett's new company manufactured products from celluloid, a combination of nitrocellulose and camphor; this was considered the first thermoplastic, and can be traced back to Parkesine in 1856 (the product's name was changed to Xylonite in 1869; celluloid was registered in 1870). Easily moulded and shaped, celluloid was employed as a replacement for ivory, and for the

Palitoy Bradgate 'Little Big Man Pony Express' and box (1975).

Palitoy Diamond Jubilee 1919–1979 commemorative brochure. Sadly, the company would only survive for another five years.

manufacture of toys and construction kits. Its major use was in the movie and photographic industries, which used only celluloid films prior to the safer acetate films introduced in the 1950s (celluloid is highly flammable).

Cascelloid's first toy appeared in 1920, and the first of a popular line of dolls in 1925.

In 1931 British Xylonite acquired the business and adopted the brand name Palitoy as a trademark. The introduction of injection moulding in 1941 improved British Xylonite's fortunes, and after the war the company continued to expand, purchasing rival doll manufacturer Chad Valley in 1978.

In 1966 Palitoy (from 1964 it was a British subsidiary of General Mills) was the UK licensee for Hasbro Industries, and was given the opportunity of releasing their enormously successful GI Joe action figure in the United Kingdom. Whilst dressing their figure in the same, mainly US uniforms, Palitoy suggested a name change, and Action Man was born.

Palitoy was bought by US food conglomerate General Mills in 1968, and formed part of the company's toy division, CPG (Creative Products Group). Alongside popular action figures such as Action Man, 'Action Force' and 'Little Big Man', in 1981 Palitoy became the home of Airfix, General Mills having recently acquired the famous brand. Airfix produced kits, toys, games, its own model railway system ('GMR' model railways), and even an action figure range, 'Airfix Eagles'.

Palitoy ceased to be an independent business in 1984 when CPG, in response to General Mills' decision to divest itself of toy businesses, closed its entire design department. In 1985 manufacturing at Palitoy also ceased, with nearly 1,000 staff facing redundancy. Airfix was sold to Humbrol in 1986.

Palitoy 'Talking Dalek' (1975).

Based on the early Mercury capsule, the Action Man space capsule was somewhat out of date when released in the UK, a year before the Apollo Moon landing (1968).

permanently separated from the rest of Cascelloid, and renamed the Palitoy Division.

In England, 1966 is not only famous for a particular World Cup win, it was also the year that the legendary Action Man hit the shops.

Action Man Hits the English Market

In England, 1966 is not only famous for a *particular* world cup win, it was also the year when the legendary Action Man hit the shops; a licensed-built version of US giant Hasbro's hit toy, GI Joe. Palitoy fought

When Action Man arrived in the UK he was clothed and equipped in exactly the same way as his American counterpart. Peaked fatigue caps would have to do. Berets would come later.

Coveted by every owner of Action Man – the 'Movable Fighting Man''s dog tag.

The Action Man *Official Equipment Manual* presented a dazzling array of vehicles and accessories – many of the larger items were special items one might anticipate at Christmas or for a birthday. Pocket money was saved to purchase the cheaper, carded accessory set.

off stiff competition from Lines Bros (parent of the famous Tri-ang brand and owners of Pedigree, who were already reaping huge rewards with 'Sindy'), and when it was launched at the Brighton Toy Fair, Action Man caused a sensation. Some commentators consider that missing out on Action Man was Lines Bros' biggest mistake.

In 1968 British Xylonite Ltd sold their Palitoy division to the US conglomerate General Mills Incorporated. A North American giant in food products, General Mills had diversified into other consumer products and had recently acquired several other toy manufacturers, including Parker Bros and Kenner. Palitoy became the centre of the General Mills UK Toy Group.

GENERAL MILLS

With perhaps one of the most varied histories of any company – as it says on the company's website, 'from flour to submarines, from toys to restaurants' – General Mills can trace its history back to 1856, when Illinois congressman Robert Smith founded the Minneapolis Milling Company. Shortly afterwards Cadwallader C. Washburn, himself also a congressman and governor of Wisconsin, acquired the company, hiring his brother William D. Washburn to assist in its development. There were six Washburn brothers, and each of them had attended President Lincoln's inauguration! Two new mills, 'A', the largest, and 'B', were the result of this early development, setting the scene for a story of continuous progress and expansion.

Interestingly, for much of its history General Mills competed with another Minnesota-based miller, Charles Pillsbury, until they finally acquired the famous home of the Pillsbury Doughboy in 2001. The company's flour mills went on to win awards and the business prospered, in 1924 even acquiring a failing radio station, WLAG, which it renamed WCCO (after the Washburn-Crosby Company).

'General Mills' itself was created in June 1928 when Washburn-Crosby President James Ford Bell merged Washburn-Crosby with twenty-eight other mills.

From 1929, General Mills' products featured box-top coupons known as Betty Crocker coupons, after the fictional character created in 1921 following a contest in the *Saturday Evening Post*. These coupons had varying points values, and were redeemable for discounts on a variety of houseware products featured in the widely distributed *Betty Crocker* catalogue. The coupons and catalogue were discontinued by the company only as recently as 2006.

General Mills became the sponsor of the popular radio show *The Lone Ranger* in 1941. The show was then brought to television. After twenty years, in 1961, their sponsorship came to an end. Since 1959, General Mills has sponsored the *Rocky and His Friends* television series, later known as *The Bullwinkle Show*. General Mills was also a sponsor of the Saturday morning cartoons, as well as the ABC Western series *The Life and Legend of Wyatt Earp*, starring Hugh O'Brian.

General Mills first ventured into toys in 1965 when it acquired Rainbow Crafts, the manufacturer of Play-Doh, the children's modelling compound, substantially cutting production costs and increasing the value of the product as they did so.

Britain's Palitoy was sold to General Mills in 1968, and formed part of the company's toy division, known as CPG (Creative Products Group) Products Corp. In 1981 when Airfix Products fell into receivership, General Mills acquired the Airfix kit range and also its GMR model railways range, charging their British subsidiary Palitoy with managing the new business. Palitoy also had responsibility for the UK rights to Meccano, acquired alongside Miro-Meccano in France following the collapse of British toy group, Tri-ang.

However, in 1984 Palitoy effectively ceased to be an independent business when CPG closed its entire design department, leaving the famous Leicestershire company as little more than just a sales and marketing operation.

In 1985, General Mills' toy division was separated from its parent and spun off as Kenner Parker Toys, Inc. Having given up toys and retailing, General Mills returned to the original focus of Cadwallader Washburn and Charles Pillsbury when they founded the business: milling and the production of fine flour.

Securing the licence for GI Joe/ Action Man had a significant effect on Palitoy's growth and prosperity. By 1978, Palitoy had approximately 1,000 employees, and in November of 1978, its sales topped £20 million for the first time in the company's history. The Palitoy factory had originally been a modest 28,000 square feet, but had now grown to nearly three times that size. The value of its production output had equally increased exponentially, from £1.2 million in 1969 to £11.6 million in 1978. By 1979 export sales had increased to £2 million, with Action Man contributing nearly 60 per cent of this total.

As we shall see, Palitoy did much more than simply reuse Hasbro's GI Joe patterns and mould tools, going on instead to enhance and, in the eyes of most enthusiasts, greatly improve the original American action figure. This was not simply the result of an improved product offering, but significantly, British families were not subjected to nightly television bulletins showing their youngsters, mostly teenage rookie soldiers, loaded on to cargo aircraft in body bags. By the late 1960s, the reality of the Vietnam War had naturally reduced the appeal of 'war toys' in the United States.

One of the 'Officers' series, like most of the German World War II outfits, the 'Action Man Panzer Captain' was much prized.

The 'Action Man Jeep and Trailer' was one of the first vehicles offered shortly after the figure appeared on the British market in 1966. Naturally it was a copy of GI Joe's World War II 'Willys Jeep'.

Palitoy's relationship with Action Man lasted from 1966 until 1983. The US moniker GI Joe ('GI' is short for 'government issue') was not thought appropriate for the British market, and a new name was sought. Allegedly, one early name suggestion was 'Ace 21' because the mannequin had twenty-one separate components…

At that time *Danger Man*, a television series starring Patrick McGoohan as secret agent John Drake, was proving especially popular in Britain, noticeably with younger audiences. Because of this, and the fact that Merrill Hassenfeld, CEO of Hasbro at the time of GI Joe's launch, had famously commanded that anyone who called the new toy a doll was risking their job, insisting on the term 'action figure' for Stan Weston instead, it is perhaps not surprising that Action Man was the British incarnation's chosen name.

Despite changing the figure's name, Palitoy retained the trio of ingenious copyright devices Hasbro had originally applied to GI Joe to thwart the emergence of knock-offs from the Far East. Consequently, the

PEDIGREE TOYS

British company Pedigree Toys is most famous for its 'Sindy' doll, which it launched in 1963 to rival Barbie. Amongst action-figure collectors, however, it is most revered for its 'Tommy Gunn' and 'Captain Scarlet' figures. A division of Lines Bros, the famous Merton-based owners of the Tri-ang brand and by the early 1960s the biggest toy company in the world, Pedigree launched Sindy in 1963; since then, though ownership of the brand has changed, the doll has sold more than 150 million units.

Introduced in 1966, the short-lived *Tommy Gunn* figure (it was discontinued in 1968) has proved to be a favourite amongst collectors. This is partly due to scarcity because of its limited production run, and because of the accuracy of uniforms and accessories. At a time when British youngsters had to content themselves with Action Man figures armed with American Armalite M-16 rifles and wearing GI Joe's M1 helmet, purchasers of 'Tommy Gunn' discovered that their 12-inch warrior fired the new FN SLR (self-loading rifle) or perhaps the 9mm Sterling SMG (submachine gun), wore 58 pattern webbing, and the new(ish) MkIV helmet on their heads.

It was rumoured that the accuracy of 'Tommy Gunn''s uniforms and equipment was facilitated by the fact that Pedigree had a mole in Britain's Ministry of Defence, who surreptitiously provided details of the latest army kit. Even though Palitoy famously improved and enhanced the design of Action Man's accessories, purists argue that the detail and accuracy of 'Tommy Gunn' components were superior. They even provided real laces for the figure's boots!

Pedigree went on to enjoy continued success with a range of figures associated with Gerry Anderson's enormously successful *Captain Scarlet and the Mysterons* television series. However, in 1971 external factors took a hand in Pedigree's future when parent Lines Bros called in the official receiver, to be broken up and shared between new businesses Rovex Tri-ang and Dunbee-Combex-Marx (DCM), who had acquired Louis Marx's British interests. DCM expected big things for Sindy in the USA – perhaps she would prove a welcome change to Barbie for American girls.

Sadly it was not to be, and the subsequent downturn of the British economy later in the 1970s ultimately contributed to the collapse of Dunbee-Combex-Marx itself, and in March 1982, Pedigree closed its newest factory in Wellingborough, Northamptonshire. Hasbro bought the rights to Sindy in 1986, but returned them to Pedigree in 1998 after sales of the doll declined. Sindy was then licensed to Vivid Imaginations, who relaunched the doll in 1999.

'Tommy Gunn' figures are now extremely rare and highly collectable, as are the subsequent 'Captain Scarlet' figurines. Boxed 'Tommy Gunn' figures, complete with literature and the figure's distinctive dog tag, can achieve top prices. Recently a 1968 Sindy doll, 'Miss Beautiful', realized more than £400 at auction.

Rare mint Pedigree 'Destiny Angel' bendy doll figure (1967).

facial scar on the figure's right cheek, the typographic copyright information on his buttock, and the figure's cunning inverted thumbnail, all remained.

Supplementary Accessory Sets

Initially Palitoy followed Hasbro's lead, and apart from changing GI Joe's name, fell in line with established plans, releasing three action figures: a soldier, sailor and pilot. These figures came dressed in the most rudimentary outfits – especially the 'Action Pilot', which came garbed in bright orange overalls with a blue US peaked fatigue cap on its head. To be honest, this was a disappointment to youthful purchasers at the time, of whom I was one, especially as the figure's box seduced us with a striking image of a jet pilot bedecked in full flying gear, including 'bone dome' and a parachute harness slung over his shoulder.

But this was the key to the success of GI Joe, Action Man and, of course, Barbie: purchasers were required to continuously acquire supplementary accessory sets if they were ever to achieve the desired effect. Current legislation would make such 'misrepresentation' difficult – today's customers have a right to expect that they will receive what is shown on the

box – and this is one of the reasons why, in the 1980s, Airfix dropped its striking Roy Cross artwork in favour of rather blander photographs of a single assembled kit, which removed any suggestion that there might be more than one aircraft, vehicle or ship in the box. To achieve a result close to the illustration of the fighter pilot shown on the GI Joe box, purchasers

ABOVE: **Probably the most popular 'Soldiers of the Century' ensemble: the 'German Stormtrooper'.**

With music by Cliff Adams, fans could even listen to the 'Action Man March' on their Dansette record player.

were obliged to buy at least three accessory packs: a flying helmet with oxygen mask, the parachute and harness, and the life vest that came complete with utility knife and scabbard.

In Britain, the introduction of Action Man made such a positive impact that the toy was voted Boys' Toy of the Year 1966 by the National Association of Toy Retailers.

Collectors might like to know that the earliest Action Man figures can be identified by the presence of flesh-colour paint on the top of the steel rivets securing the articulation of limbs, and which provide mounting points for the complex internal web of elastic cords that enabled any temporarily dislocated arms and legs to return to their proper position. Later figures dispensed with such cosmetic enhancement, and rivet tops were left in bare metal.

Early on, Palitoy introduced Action Man stars, a loyalty scheme that encouraged purchasers to '... get another "Action Man", a "Royal Canadian Mounted

Footy fans weren't left out. In the 1960s West Ham fans could even purchase an Action Man figure of one of their team's players.

This 'Action Man Tank Commander' demonstrates just how useless these warriors were when they tried to hold one of their weapons properly!

Action Man Design Improvements

Whilst it was Hasbro that pioneered the installation within GI Joe's torso of a drawstring-operated, amplified tape voicebox (later replaced by a miniature disc), Palitoy were the first to address the 12-inch fighting man's most glaring design fault – the fact that despite being able to call upon an almost unlimited armoury of rifles, machine guns and pistols, neither GI Joe nor Action Man could easily hold any of them in the manner that real soldiers take for granted! As all true enthusiasts will testify, Action Man's wrists would easily be dislocated when trying to encourage the figure to hold a weapon in anything approaching an offensive posture.

Fortunately, in 1971 (Bill) William A.G. Pugh, Palitoy's Director of Design, Research and Development, came up with a solution to the failings in Action Man's posture, and 'gripping hands' were born. Now, thanks to the introduction of a new plastic formulation, Kraton, a material suggested by Palitoy's Chief Designer Bob Brechin, Action Man could aim his rifle properly and target an opponent directly ahead of him. Until he acquired 'gripping hands', because his weapons had to be carried transversely, across the body in the manner that those holding pugil sticks or quarterstaffs

'Gripping hands', a Palitoy innovation, at last put an end to Action Man's inept ability to hold things. They were invented by the director of the Design Department, Bill Pugh, and designed and sculpted by chief designer Bob Brechin, who used his left hand as a model. A thimble was provided with each boxed figure to protect its fingers when changing its outfit.

Policeman" uniform, or an "Action Man Guard Dog" *free*!' Once purchasers had snipped enough of the tiny red five-pointed symbols from Action Man packaging and pasted them on to a collector's card, they could be redeemed for a free gift. How many of us remember receiving 'Brutus', the 'Action Man Guard Dog', which could be acquired for a very modest ten stars?

generally deport themselves, Action Man could really only shoot anyone standing to his immediate left or right.

However, because it was so flexible, the new plastic used for Action Man's hands meant that fingers and thumbs were liable to damage if they caught on the inseams of jacket sleeves (dressing and undressing Action Man was always a trial – remember trying

The '**Action Man French Resistance Fighter**' first appeared in 1968 and came complete with a beret, sweater, trousers, boots (short black), a Lebel revolver in a shoulder holster, knife and grenades. He could even sport a Croix de Guerre medal, though it is unlikely he would have worn it in the field.

to get the little chap's combat boots on and off?): consequently, 'Gripping Hands Action Men' came complete with a nylon thimble, provided to protect exposed thumbs, preventing them from breaking each time the figure was dressed or disrobed.

Actually, a year earlier, Bill Pugh was responsible for another Action Man first – realistic flock hair. The original GI Joe and Action Man figures featured moulded hairstyles, painted either black, brown or yellow (blonde). From 1970 onwards however, Action Man could be purchased with either a blonde or brown/auburn mixed flock head of hair. In 1971 the 'Sailor' and 'Adventurer' figures even sported flocked beards.

Innovation wasn't only the province of Palitoy – many ideas emanated stateside, and Hasbro US was notably responsible for 'Eagle Eyes', a development introduced in 1977 that enabled youngsters to direct their action figure's gaze by manipulating a cunning lever in the back of his neck.

New Design Lines for the Domestic Market

At first, Action Man was dressed and equipped with American uniforms, arms and accessories, identical to those available for GI Joe back in his place of birth. To the dismay of British youngsters, these were far more suited to a US barrack block or armoury.

Uniform and Equipment Sets

The absence of any identifiable British uniforms and equipment was something Tri-ang's Pedigree exploited in full, with their new 'Tommy Gunn' figure that was introduced in the same year that Action Man made his debut. Whilst Action Man wore US-style OG (Olive Green) 107 fatigues and sported an M1 helmet when he wasn't wearing his fatigue cap, 'Tommy Gunn' was clad in British 1949 pattern battledress, and wore the distinctive Mk III 'turtle' helmet that was first used in combat by British and empire troops on D-Day. 'Tommy Gunn' was also armed with the new 9mm-calibre Sterling sub machine-gun and the 7.62-calibre FN SLR (self-loading rifle). Initially, Britain's Action Man had to be satisfied with fielding only US weapons such as the M1 Garand .30-calibre rifle, or M3 .45 'Grease Gun'.

Curiously, Palitoy never fully addressed the lack of contemporary British army equipment for Action Man, but the Coalville team was responsible for a great many original uniform and equipment sets, and they also designed a range of vehicles, which even included a Snowcat-tracked vehicle used for Arctic warfare. They also designed and manufactured a fantastic replica of a Scorpion tank, which Palitoy described as having: '...real hatch openings for two "Action Man" soldiers... while moving tracks

Vintage mint-on-card 'Indian Brave' set.

and revolving turret will add real excitement to the armoured division.'

With the domestic market in mind, by 1970 Palitoy had released a range of admirably detailed uniforms of famous regiments. The official equipment manual supplied with each new outfit claimed they had been designed 'with the assistance of the regiments concerned', and they certainly were superb replicas, especially the Life Guard, Blues & Royals and 17th/21st Lancers outfits, which came with chromed helmets or Uhlan's czapkas as appropriate. An accessory set that included a chromed cuirass (breastplate) both front and back, and came with a chromed sabre and scabbard, was also available to further enhance the Life Guard figure.

From 1972, a magnificent horse, sculpted by Bill Pugh, was also made available. This stunning replica not only complemented the cavalry of the Household Division, but was also ideal for use with the Action Man 7th Cavalry figure. An Indian Pony was also available for use with the Action Man 'Indian Chief' and 'Indian Brave' outfits.

In distinctive packaging emblazoned with a striking Union Jack, the new 'Famous British Uniforms' range also included a selection of paratrooper figures, amongst which a classic Parachute Regiment figure clad in the unit's unique Denison smock, wearing one of the hard-won maroon berets on his head, immediately proved enormously popular.

For those youngsters – or their parents – with deeper pockets, a fantastic red devil paratrooper was also available. Dressed in

'Fighting soldiers from the sky, Fearless men who jump and die': 'Action Man Green Beret' outfit in all its glory.

One of the rarer figures, the 'Action Man Space Ranger Commando' from 1983.

'Zargonite Space Pirate', the deadly enemy of the Space Rangers (1982).

'Space Ranger Space Gun', the purchase of which gained a single Action Man star towards something else.

bright red overalls and wearing a white crash helmet (emblazoned with 'Action Man Red Devil' on the front) and tinted goggles, this set featured a working parachute that was appropriately finished in red, white and blue segments.

Just like early GI Joes, and the Marx figures that were even more susceptible to failure, Action Man's plastic composition was also prone to fatigue, which manifested itself most notably as conspicuous stress fractures close to the joints and fixing pegs.

Whilst it was great fun to chuck the Red Devil skywards and wait for the parachute to deploy and the figure to float back down to Earth, any mishaps could end in disaster, as the stress of a heavy landing might lead to damage, possibly resulting in unavoidable amputation. Action Man's brightly coloured parachute did, however, mean that any wayward Red Devils perched high up in trees could be readily located!

In 1973 Palitoy finally attended to the absence of modern British army uniforms and equipment throughout the Action Man range. The Action Man Basic Soldier now came dressed in an olive drab wool jersey and olive drab fatigues, and wore a black beret on his head. Furthermore, after selling in disappointing quantities compared to the volume sales that Action Man enjoyed, in 1968 Pedigree's 'Tommy Gunn' figure was discontinued, leaving the way clear for Palitoy's fighting soldier. And now, for the first time, Action Man was armed with modern British kit, noticeably an FN SLR, though unfortunately, like its 'Tommy Gunn' predecessor, this miniature was prone to damage, its delicate scale barrel frequently snapping.

The 'Action Man Talking Commander'

In 1968 the 'Action Man Talking Commander' hit British toy shops. An officer figure, he came clad in a smart, red-banded peaked cap, with a scarf setting off his jumper, and he sported a belted pistol in a holster around his waist. A tug of his drawstring activated one of five random messages. (GI Joe found his

Alongside other Household Cavalry and British ceremonial regimental uniforms, by 1970 those fans with deeper pockets might possess the magnificent 'Action Man 17th/21st Lancer' and his horse.

voice earlier than this, and when, as an army child I lived in Hong Kong in the mid-1960s, I remember being enthralled by hearing the American voice of my action figure shout, amongst other things, 'Enemy planes, hit the dirt!')

Capable of issuing eight commands at random, depending on how far out you pulled the cord, Action Man's repertoire included such classics as 'This is your commander speaking', 'Enemy aircraft, action stations', 'Volunteer needed for a special mission', 'Enemy in sight: range 1000', 'Action Man patrol fall in', 'Hold your fire until I give the order', 'Mortar attack, dig in', and finally, 'Commander to base, request support fire'.

Action Man Vehicles

A wide range of vehicles provided Action Man with the mobility he required to exercise his full potential

To commemorate the 40th anniversary of the Battle of Britain, in 1980 Palitoy released a superb 'Action Man Fighter Pilot' figure.

on the battlefield. At first, these were just licensed copies of GI Joe's jeeps, ammunition trailers and mobile searchlights, but very soon an exciting range of more bespoke vehicles emerged from Palitoy's Leicestershire design department. Some of them were scale replicas, though for practicality, not to Action Man's 1:6 scale. They included current British Army vehicles, and alongside the Scorpion tank there was a Spartan armoured personnel carrier, Ferret armoured car, even a 105mm light gun and air portable Land Rover and trailer.

With Action Man armed to the teeth, it would have been unreasonable to expect his adversaries to put up a fair fight unless they were similarly equipped. Therefore, to level the playing field somewhat, Action Man's almost inevitably German foe could also call upon a range of military hardware, including a passable interpretation of the Wehrmacht's jeep, the VW-built Kübelwagen, and a now most desirable German Afrika Korps motorcycle and sidecar combination.

As they had with GI Joe/ Action Man's physiognomy, Hasbro and Palitoy's competitors also attempted to copy his vehicles. Here, without resorting to direct

imitation, it was a bit easier to grab a piece of Hasbro's action (no pun intended). If the vehicle was of 1:6 scale and marketed as 'suitable for "GI Joe" or "Action Man" figures', emulators would get away with it.

Some rivals, such as Britain's Cherilea – a toy company founded in 1946 by Messrs Cherrington and Leaver, who had formerly worked for the famous toy soldier company Johillco – went that bit further and produced vehicles of real quality, most notably their Kettenkraftrad, the German army's ingenious motorcycle/half-track combination.

Hasbro's action figures weren't confined to land vehicles: they could also take to the air. There was 'Action Man's Pursuit Craft', a kind of microlight with floats, that was 'capable of seeking adventure on land, sea and in the air'. There was even a helicopter 'with working rotor and winch', into which Action Man fitted snugly. The stout box warned purchasers that the helicopter *will not fly*, but I doubt this prevented many youngsters from launching the toy from their bedroom windows.

It didn't end there, and Action Man could also go underwater. Actually, dressed in the Deep-Sea Diver helmet and rubberized outfit, he had been capable

Issued within the 'Officers' series, the 'Battle of Britain Fighter Pilot' outfit came on a vacuum-formed 'blister-pack' card.

'Battle of Britain Luftwaffe' and 'RAF' figures from 1980, up close and personal!

of remaining submerged for ages, but now with the addition of 'Sea Wolf', 'a one-man submarine that could dive and surface by remote control', he could really explore the hidden depths of the bath tub.

Action Man's International Success

GI Joe and Action Man's success wasn't limited to the United States and the United Kingdom. Soon, all of Europe was in the thrall of this action figure, and continental manufacturers snapped up the GI Joe licence from Hasbro with indecent haste.

In Spain, Action Man was rebranded 'Geyperman'. In France he was called 'Action Joe'. In Germany he had become part of the 'Action Team' that comprised no-nonsense characters such as 'Hard Rock' and 'John Steel'. Production of 'Geyperman' ended in 1982, but such was the figure's popularity that Spain's Hobbycrash produced limited re-releases, some of which were restricted to only 250 units of each figure. Consequently, some of these twenty-first-century editions are now as valuable as many of those from forty years ago.

The GI Joe concept had struck a chord with youngsters across the globe.

Australia's Kenbrite, manufacturer of the antipodean favourite, 'Digger the Dog', grabbed a GI Joe licence, as did Takara and Tsukuda in Japan. Curiously, Palitoy also struck a deal with Australian toy importer Toltoys, who renamed Action Man 'Falcon'.

'Action Girl' – 'She moves in such an exciting world!' – was born in 1971 and remained in production until 1977.

In Mexico, GI Joe was licensed to Lili-Ledy, where he become one of the 'Hombres de Acción' ('Men of Action').

In partnership with Lion Rock, Mego's manufacturing arm which they employed to distribute their products in Europe, Italian toy company Polistil (initially founded as Politoys in 1960, and better known today for their association with diecast metal and plastic vehicles) secured the rights from Hasbro to produce versions of both GI Joe and Action Man well into the late 1970s. This made it possible for European enthusiasts to obtain both figures easily, something action-figure collectors in the United Kingdom found more difficult to do, 12-inch GI Joes being a rarity in the UK. Polistil's 'Action Team' and 'Action Girls' figures are now highly sought after by collectors, especially since Polistil ceased trading in 1993.

Bob Brechin: Developing Action Man, the Inside Story

Keith Melville told me he was in regular contact with Bob Brechin, Palitoy's Chief Designer – I mentioned

An unlikely assembly: Action Man Japanese, Australian, British and German soldiers lined up in front of a rare plywood 'Command HQ'.

him earlier in this narrative in relation to the composition of Action Man's 'gripping hands'. Keith said that Mr Brechin was not only in charge of Action Man, but that he currently runs the Action Man History Group. Keith advised me he could be found on Facebook, and sure enough, it was via social media that I elicited Bob Brechin's help.

'I joined Palitoy in 1967, the year after the launch of "Action Man",' Bob told me. 'I left in 1984, the last year before the licence was returned to Hasbro, and as a result, the entire design department was made redundant.'

Bob told me that just before he joined Palitoy, riding high on the success of their 'Sindy' doll, which had been selling extremely well since its launch in 1968, Pedigree Dolls & Toys, a subsidiary of British toy giant Lines Bros (Tri-ang), had decided to compete head-on with GI Joe (Action Man) by releasing their own soldier figure, 'Tommy Gunn'. He pointed out that, unlike Palitoy, who benefited from Hasbro's substantial US investment in the design and tooling of GI Joe and only had to make copies from existing moulds, Pedigree, obliged to start from scratch, was faced with an enormous initial financial outlay.

'This meant that a big chunk of money went into design and development, leaving little left to promote "Tommy Gunn",' he told me. Lack of promotion was clearly one of the reasons that Tri-ang's competitor was so short-lived, disappearing off the shelves less than three years after its inception. This is one of the reasons that surviving 'Tommy Gunn' figures and accessories are today so coveted and expensive.

Bob told me that he was soon tasked with widening the scope of Action Man by developing sports and adventure outfits and accessories, something the American originators of GI Joe never embraced. He recalled:

> I was made Chief Designer as the department got bigger and so had more designers and enjoyed the support of a model maker. Obviously, I wasn't there when the staff first met GI Joe, and I know a lot of them thought that boys wouldn't play with a doll. I suppose my favourite memories are developing the ceremonials, and especially being entertained

at the Household Cavalry barracks in Whitehall by their commanding officer, who let us take away a full uniform and tack for the horse we were modelling for our figure.

Another highlight Bob remembers was being shown round the 17th and 21st Lancers museum at Belvoir Castle: 'By none less than the Duke of Rutland!' He also recalled that: 'Designing the Scorpion Tank was fun – especially the visit to Alvis in Coventry and getting to ride around in it!' Already well known for their civilian automobiles and armoured cars, Alvis was also a leading manufacturer of racing cars and aircraft engines. Bob explained:

> The GI Joe and Action Man stories are different, but ran parallel for a while. They (Hasbro) came up with 'Talking Commander' but we transformed the figure, adding realistic hair and 'gripping hands', and these additions allowed the marketing department to promote such developments on the packs and in TV adverts at regular intervals, which helped to keep the concept alive. Of course, Hasbro had to go one better with 'Eagle Eyes' just before they withdrew GI Joe, which we in turn adopted for Action Man.

Bob also told me that another of the things he was especially satisfied with was employing Greg Hughes, who joined Palitoy as a product designer in 1978 after applying to a job advertisement. 'This was a good move because he came up with designs for "Special Team", which was a departure from basically copying historical or existing uniforms.' Palitoy's 'Action Man Special Teams', the last iteration of the traditional 12-inch figure – 'Today's Best Equipped Fighting Force' – were imaginative, fictitious figures available in sets such as 'Missile Assault', 'Arctic Assault' and 'Ground Assault'.

'I particularly enjoyed the development of Action Force, which we did from scratch,' said Bob. 'Especially the "Baron Ironblood" redesign, where I was able to use my imagination.'

'Action Force' was Palitoy's answer to the enormous success of the smaller 3-inch figures that Kenner had

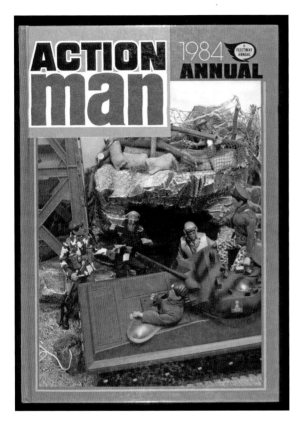

The Action Man franchise was supported by regular annuals. This one dates from 1984.

sold by the million since they acquired the 'Star Wars' franchise in 1977, and 'Baron Ironblood', their nemesis, was the leader of the piratical 'Red Shadows'.

'And of course there was "Roboskull", my ultimate fantasy toy,' Bob remembered, recalling the fantastical air/space fighter, which had vertical take-off and landing (VTOL) capabilities thanks to the variable position of its engines. 'Roboskull' graced the pages of *Battle Action Force*, the comic that documented the adventures of Action Force and its enemies. The vehicle survived the transition from 'Action Force and the Red Shadows' into Hasbro's later 'GI Joe Cobra' 3-inch figure range. Said Bob proudly:

> Over the years we transformed the original GI Joe figure into a real British icon. There were Palitoy additions such as the 'Land Rover' and the '105mm Gun', notwithstanding all the British regiments we introduced. The name Action Man was a master stroke because it allowed us to make him a real man of action in other theatres than just the military.

In an interview with the Victoria & Albert Museum of Childhood in May 2010, Bob Brechin went on record to tell researchers Ieuan Hopkins and Sarah Wood more about his time at Palitoy with Action Man.

The Action Man 30th anniversary gift set was released in 1996. By then the original 1960s mould tools had disappeared, and this new figure had a somewhat more heavily set physique than the original Action Man.

Although General Mills had bought the company, Bob told his interviewers that they 'left Palitoy to their own devices', giving the designers there freedom to develop Action Man as they saw fit.

'They (Palitoy) just had to report to the parent company (Hasbro) on what they were doing, just to get agreement,' he revealed, acknowledging the latitude Palitoy enjoyed. 'The turnover was tremendous – "Action Man" was probably about two-thirds of Palitoy's income.'

Another development was the hair on the GI Joe figure, which on the original was simply painted on and not sufficiently realistic for Bob or his boss, Bill Pugh, director of the design department. Bob explained that whilst Mr Pugh was watching BBC television's *Tomorrow's World*, his attention was caught by a demonstration of a process called 'flocking'.

> So he phoned the BBC and found out who the company was that was doing it, and rang them up and invited them in. The chap turned up in a car with flock all over it in different tones of blue. He drove into the car park with this car. He came into the office and those sitting there, including Bill and myself, watched as he got this box, and from it, took out a full tea set, tea pot, milk jug, cups and saucers, all flocked in different colours, so they're like hairy cups and saucers. Then Bill got out the Action Man head and held it up to him and said, 'Can you flock that?' 'Well, give me a few and I'll take them away,' he answered, and went away before returning with the process to do it.

Exhibiting the flocked hair created by Bill Pugh, Palitoy's Director of Design, this is 'Tom Stone', the first black figure in the Action Man range, who appeared in 1977. Based on a Hasbro design from the USA, he had a more muscular body than other Palitoy figures.

Apparently, the electrostatic process that achieved this realistic hair growth relied on attaching a positive electrode inside the hollow head of the Action Man to be treated, and then simply putting the head inside a box packed with tiny nylon fibres, all negatively charged – the head would be positively charged. Consequently, the fibres would be magically attracted and jump on to the pre-glued head. 'And that's how the "Action Man" hair was invented by Bill Pugh,' Bob disclosed cheerfully.

The advent of the three-day week during the 1973 oil crisis naturally had a detrimental effect on the production of plastic, a material derived from oil, and inevitably this had a knock-on effect on toy production, as Bob advised:

> So we were looking at ways of cheapening toys – with regard to plastic, I mean – which is why 'Star Wars' made a killing really, because the 'Star Wars' figures are only 3¾ inches high, whereas Action Man is 12 inches high. There was also a toy called 'Little Big Man', which we did, which was about 4 or 5 inches high, to reduce the amount of plastic. The Action Man 12-inch figure still carried on right to 1984, but we decided to do a very similar figure – well, the same size as the Star Wars ones – which we called 'Action Force'.

Bob revealed that 'Action Force' figures were manufactured in the same way as Kenner's 'Star Wars' figures – a sonic welded body, with the arms, legs and head trapped between the two clamshell-like torso mouldings.

Just quite how much freedom Palitoy enjoyed with the GI Joe franchise is evident by the company's production of items aimed rather parochially at the domestic market. These included the 'Action Cricketer Set', which first appeared in 1968 but had disappeared from the range by 1970. This, now rare set, included a cricketer figure dressed in whites, V-neck jumper and cap with badge, who stood, bat in hand, ready to protect his wicket.

Further Developments for Action Man

Palitoy hadn't simply appropriated the GI Joe licence:

Dr X (Count Laszlo Huszar II) arrived in the Action Man range in 1993. A scientist bent on world domination, he was also the leader of the terroristic 'Council of Doom'.

With Action Man moving away from his traditional militaristic roots, in 1996 the 'Sport Extreme' figure made his debut.

with Hasbro's acquiescence they had embraced it vigorously, and since the first moment they acquired it, had raced ahead to enhance the product. Their efforts were acknowledged with yet another award when, in 1975, the National Association of Toy Retailers honoured them with a 'Ten Year Gold Award'. In recognition of this accolade, a gold sticker was added to boxes distributed during this period.

The 1977 official catalogue included four new figures, three of which were variations on the standard Action Man: a cyborg 'Atomic Man' (influenced by *The Six Million Dollar Man*); a black commando, 'Tom Stone'; a red and silver superhero 'Bullet Man'; and finally a fantasy figure inspired by pre-historic hominids, named 'The Intruder'.

In 1978, with the advent of a new, more muscular body shape, Palitoy developed Action Man even further. The voice-over on a new television advertisement announced:

> As storm clouds gather over Mrs Roger's garden, the Action Man gang assemble for the big parade. It's an impressive display of military muscle – and speaking of muscle, just look at Action Man's new, fully posable physique. It's 'chest out and eyes right'

as the top brass take the salute. They know that Action Man, with his dynamic new physique, is ready for action!

The television commercial above ended with a message revealing the recommended purchase price of Action Man figures, which in 1978 could each be acquired individually for £3.75 (a considerable sum for a toy at the time), or in elaborate combination sets for as much as £7.50. This incarnation of Action Man featured improved 'gripping hands', manufactured from a more robust plastic composition (collectors will testify that the early hands have a tendency to discolour over time), together with the movable 'Eagle Eyes'. The fact that this version also seemed to be wearing a pair of blue underpants caused some amusement amongst owners.

Though risky, the opportunity to tie in with a popular movie franchise or television series can generate significant returns, and toy manufacturers generally jump at the chance of such collaborations. Telling the story of the many escape attempts by Allied prisoners of war held at the supposedly escape-proof Oflag IV-C during World War II, *Colditz*, a British television series that aired on the BBC between 1972

From 1966 a 'Star Collection Scheme' operated, whereby purchasers were required to snip stars from packaging and stick them to the Star Award Card before redeeming a gift. 'Brutus', the 'Mastiff Guard Dog', could be secured with only ten such stars.

and 1974, was enormously successful. It didn't take long for toy manufacturers to acquire licences – Parker, the games division of Palitoy, who had recently produced an Action Man board game, quickly released an even more elaborate one co-designed by Major Pat Reid, one of the few inmates to successfully escape from the forbidding castle. Construction kit manufacturer Airfix even produced an 18-inch free-flying glider.

But in 1974 Palitoy went one better and released the 'Action Man Escape from Colditz Set', which included the uniforms of the Escape Officer and a German Sentry (but no figures), plus a range of Colditz accessories, including a self-assembly German cardboard

sentry box with barrier. Forged escape papers to facilitate the inmates' escape were also included.

Peter Allen at Palitoy

Following the construction kit company's collapse and liquidation early in 1980, after nearly two decades as kit designer with Airfix, Peter Allen was fortunate enough to find himself back in work and still at Airfix. But now he was employed at their new home in Leicestershire with Palitoy, who were tasked by US conglomerate General Mills, who had just

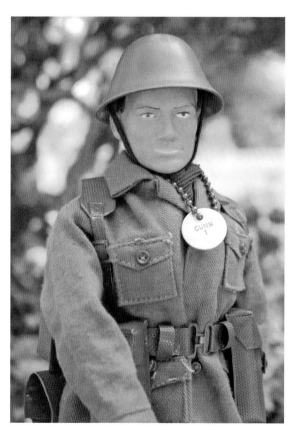

Pedigree Toys Ltd's 'Tommy Gunn' was Britain's answer to Action Man. Unlike Palitoy's figure, which was a facsimile of America's GI Joe, 'Tommy Gunn' was garbed and equipped with contemporary (for 1966) British army uniforms and equipment.

This back view of 'Tommy Gunn' reveals just how accurate his equipment was. Wearing '58 pattern webbing and the new(ish) MkIV helmet, he could be armed with either the new FN SLR (self-loading rifle) or the 9mm Sterling SMG (submachine gun). Action Man had to rely on the US ArmaLite AR-15 assault rifle or M-1 carbine.

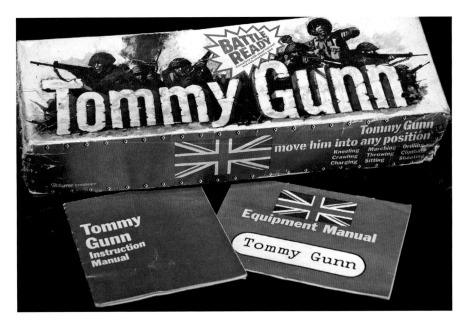

As rare as hens' teeth: original vintage 'Tommy Gunn' figure in its packaging with accompanying leaflets.

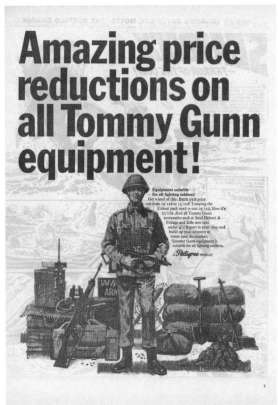

This full-page advertisement from a 1960s boys' comic promised tantalizing price reductions, and to anyone of my generation who can still convert 'old money' to decimal, makes one yearn for yesteryear.

bought Airfix from the receivers, with reviving the famous kit company. I asked Peter what it was like to now be based at the famous home of Action Man.

When the receivers sold Airfix, all the staff were made redundant, but within a matter of days three of us were offered permanent positions; my offer was to set up and manage a new Airfix Design Department reporting to the Director of Design and Development at Palitoy, John Hawkes. As John had been Head of Design in Airfix's Toys & Games R & D Department, we knew each other well and naturally I was happy to accept the position. I recruited two Airfix kit designers (David Reed and David Wick) to join me at Palitoy.

We shared a very large office with two 'Mainline' train designers, but we operated as two separate departments. Across the passage was the Action Man and Toy design team. Within a few weeks I recruited a third designer from Matchbox.

Initially the Airfix team were treated with a degree of reserve, as our salaries were based on London rates not Leicester ones. There was also a degree of resentment against me because my position was at a new level, which included a very good company car.

For the first year we worked solely on Airfix

Tommy Gunn—British Fighting Soldier

You've seen him on TV! 11 inches tall. Move him into any battle position. Comes to you in basic combat kit, already armed with a Sterling sub-machine gun.

Also Available:
FIRST AID PACK (11 TG 01) 17/9
ALL ROUND DEFENCE PACK (11 TG 02) 20/2
PARATROOP PACK (11 TG 05) 22/3
HELMET AND FOLIAGE (11 TG 52) 5/-
PARATROOP BERET AND KNIFE (11 TG 55) 5/7
SELF-LOADING RIFLE (11 TG 56) 6/-
GRENADES AND BAYONET (11 TG 54) 5/7
STERLING SUB-MACHINE CARBINE (11 TG 57) 6/-
SLEEPING BAG (11 TG 58) 8/-
BADGES OF RANK AND MEDALS (11 TG 53) 4/7
SANDBAGS AND ENTRENCHING TOOL (11 TG 51) 5/-
BIVOUAC TENT (11 TG A1) 20/2

A PEDIGREE PRODUCT

Despite the somewhat dubious colour of his lips, armed with his state-of-the-art, Belgian-made FN SLR, this 'Tommy Gunn Guardsman' is battle ready.

'You've seen him on TV!' – though it would, of course, have been on a tiny black and white set. Nevertheless, viewers of the television campaign and readers of this advertisement would have been eager for any news about 'Tommy Gunn, the British Fighting Soldier'.

products, supplementing our team with freelance ex-Airfix designers as required, but kit sales had started to decline, as had demand for Action Man, Palitoy's other major product. Fortuitously for all of us, then came the Falklands War, which boosted sale of both kits and action figures. The joke around the company was that General Mills, who owned Palitoy, must have engineered the Anglo-Argentine conflict to increase sales!

Prior to joining Airfix, our director John Hawkes had been with Matchbox, and whilst there had designed and introduced a range of small-jointed Action figures; however, the range was not a great success. Having joined Airfix, he proposed a range of similarly small figures, but again these did not prove to be a high-volume range. However, when

John joined Palitoy, his range of smaller action figures really fired up the market, and became a resounding success. The Palitoy toy range also had a product line called 'Strawberry Shortcake', and we received a delivery of our military figures that smelled of strawberries. The Far East manufacturer asked us to market them, but the reason given for rejection was that we could not have the SAS scented with strawberries!

Whilst at Palitoy, the Airfix designers started working on a range of Action Man vehicles, the initial designs for which were created by Raffo and Pape.

A notable prototype for one of these, the 'Wolf Pack Land Rover', is now in the collection of the V & A Museum of Childhood. The design of this vehicle was commissioned for the new 1984 'Action Man Wolf Pack' range. Unfortunately, this and all other designs that were adapted and designed in-house by the Palitoy design team never went into production. Though they were displayed at the 1984 Toy Fair soon afterwards, the design department was shut down and it all came to an end.

Peter recalled another fascinating story from this period, telling me that when Pope John Paul II came to the United Kingdom in May 1982 and made the first visit by a reigning Pope, one enterprising lady in the West Country decided to buy Action Man figures and sell them dressed as the Pope. Apparently, Palitoy gently advised her that this was perhaps not a viable project.

After a few years with Palitoy, Peter found himself once again looking for a new position. General Mills had entered the toy business in 1965 with the purchase of Rainbow Crafts, manufacturers of Play-Doh; twenty years later, in 1985, General Mills decided to divest itself of its toy division CPG, which became Kenner Parker Toys, Inc. Kenner, in turn, also decided to pull out of the construction kit market, selling Airfix to Humbrol in 1986. Hasbro acquired what was left of General Mills' toy interests.

Following his time at Palitoy, Peter joined Milton Bradley, working from their offices in Richmond upon Thames. Around this time MB was in the process of being acquired by Hasbro, ending 124 years of family ownership. Very soon Peter relocated again, and, with the title of Design and Development Manager, was installed in Hasbro's smart new premises in Stockley Park, in Uxbridge, Middlesex. Whilst at Hasbro, Peter was reacquainted with Action Man; he told me:

> In the 1990s Hasbro relaunched Action Man in Europe, achieving good sales figures. During 1998 and 1999 we were planning to launch a range of F1 cars in 1:32 and 1:12 scale, our star driver being Jacques Villeneuve; we also planned to market a range of 'Action Driver' figures.

The 1990s were the high point of Canadian racing driver Jacques Villeneuve's professional career. The son of Formula One driver Gilles Villeneuve, Jacques

won the 1995 CART Championship, the 1995 Indianapolis 500, and the 1997 Formula One World Championships. Driving for Peugeot, he went on to compete in the 2007 and 2008 Le Mans 24 Hours, jumping to NASCAR in between. Villeneuve's distinctive multi-

The only one in the world: surviving 'Action Man Jacques Villeneuve' prototype figure with unique head sculpt.

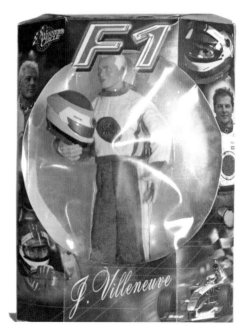

And how the 'Jacques Villeneuve' figure might have looked, if it had ever reached the shelves.

coloured helmet remained unchanged for his entire professional career. Said Peter: 'We produced just one "mock-up" driver figure, the bespoke head sculpt for which was created by Paul Gillingham and approved by Jacques Villeneuve himself.'

The figure's overalls were also especially made and embroidered by 'Christine', who worked for Peter. The driver's iconic helmet was also faithfully reproduced in miniature. I was privileged to get sight of the Jacques Villeneuve figure, and took the photographs of this very rare artefact, shown in this book. Things never progressed beyond the prototype stage because in 1999 all work on the range ceased.

Whilst talking to Peter specifically about action figures for a change – for years I've badgered him for information about plastic construction kits – he thought back to his first position in the toy industry when he worked for the legendary Lines Bros, owners of the world-famous Tri-ang brand.

Released in 1977, 'The Intruder' was Action Man's Neanderthal nemesis, and was often joined by the equally monstrous 'Gargon'.

> In my early days with them, it was the talk that Walter Lines turned down the franchise for GI Joe as he said boys did not play with dolls. The name also was unacceptable, as 'G.I.' stood for 'Government Issue', which would have meant nothing to British children. The American GIs were resented in the UK – in fact it was said there were three things wrong with them: they were over-paid, over-sexed and over here. To put the name GI Joe on the toy would have caused the death of the product.

Peter told me that when senior members of staff involved with Action Man left the Hasbro, some of them were presented with 1:6 miniatures of themselves. When he retired, Peter was the lucky recipient of one such bespoke action figure.

movies had proved consistently popular, culminating with *Star Wars* in 1977, which lifted the genre to new heights. Therefore it is no surprise that Palitoy attempted to capitalize on this phenomenon with the release of their own futuristic offerings. In 1980 Action Man 'Space Rangers' and 'Space Pirates' hit the shops, along with 'Rom the Robot' and a range of accessories that included 'Spacewalk' backpacks and a variety of laser weapons. 'Captain Zargon', the leader of the 'Space Pirates', presented a particularly impressive figure.

Presaging the later success of Marvel's 'He-Man', sitting astride 'Gargon, Beast from the Future of the Time enemies', was Action Man's nemesis, the aforementioned 'Intruder, Master of Time'. He made a frighteningly alternative opponent to the humanoid 'Space Pirates'.

Action Figures for the Early 1980s

Sci-Fi Figures and Accessory Sets

Ever since 1968's *2001: A Space Odyssey*, several sci-fi

'Action Man Sharpshooter'

In 1981, the final incarnation of Palitoy's figure the 'Action Man Sharpshooter' was available in toy shops. At last the figure had neck articulations, which enabled Action Man to aim his rifle properly. He was expensive, however, costing nearly £5, a not inconsiderable price at a time when the average weekly wage was £110.

SAS Figures and Accessory Sets

On 5 May 1980 the SAS stormed the Iranian Embassy in London's South Kensington, and brought a week-long siege to a dramatic end. The action was watched avidly by television audiences around the world, and breathed fresh life into a British Special Forces unit that many hadn't heard of since their adventures in the Libyan desert in World War II. It also provided Palitoy with the motivation to release a range of suitably themed SAS figures and accessory sets a year or so later.

Clad in black overalls, over which a bullet-proof vest was worn, and with a grey cloth hood over

The 'Action Man SAS Parachute Attack' set came with a working parachute.

The Iranian Embassy siege ended with the SAS successfully storming the building in Prince's Gate, South Kensington, on 5 May 1980 and made the, until then secretive, regiment world-famous. Palitoy rode the zeitgeist releasing a range of SAS figures including these 'SAS Commander' and 'Special Operations' figures.

his head, his face further obscured by a black gas mask, the Heckler & Koch machine-gun-wielding 'SAS Commander' figure was a perfect tribute to the regiment. The new range was complemented by other well-designed sets such as the 'SAS Beachhead Attack', 'SAS Airstrike', 'SAS Underwater Attack', 'SAS Parachute Attack' (with working parachute) and 'SAS Secret Mission'.

A Last Hurrah

For we Brits, Action Man had at last divorced himself from his US-centric appearance of yesteryear, and along with other 'patriotic' releases, such as 1980's 'Battle of Britain Fighter Pilot' and the new 'Helicopter Pilot', this provided some real home-grown toy value.

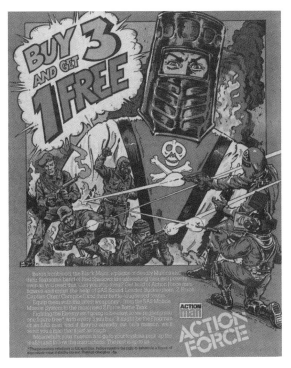

The latest attacks of 'Baron Youngblood' have forced the government to expand 'Action Force'. Adding to the crack teams of SAS and Z Force, 'Action Force' is now in space ready to defend any threat to the Earth's future with 'Space Force'. Operating from their 'Cosmic Cruiser', this top team is sure to outmanoeuvre even 'Baron Youngblood' and his 'Laser Exterminator'.

'Baron Youngblood, the Black Major', a plague of deadly 'Mutons' and their fearsome band of 'Red Shadows', are unleashing their evil powers even as you read this. Can you stop them? Get hold of 'Action Force' mini figures and enlist the help of 'SAS Squad Leader Buckingham', 'Z Force Captain Grant Campbell' and their battle-toughened teams.

'Action Force' figures, Palitoy's answer to the smaller 'Star Wars' figures that had proved so popular, were introduced in 1982. The 1980 Iranian Embassy siege and the Parachute regiment's engagement in May 1982 at Goose Green during the Falklands War, made the choice of an 'SAS Squad Leader' and '2 Para Soldier' highly appropriate.

'Action Force' – a smaller action figure based on Action Man – first appeared in 1982, mimicking the success that Kenner was enjoying with its 3-inch 'Star Wars' figures. SAS figures were naturally included in the range, and have now become very collectable.

Sadly, these figures were to be a last hurrah, for a while at least, because in 1984 Palitoy effectively ceased trading when its parent company, CPG, closed its entire design department, leaving only a sales and marketing operation. In May 1985 most manufacturing at Palitoy came to an end: 327 staff in manufacturing and distribution out of 585 were made redundant, and manufacturing was shifted overseas.

Hasbro's New Toy Line

Hasbro had introduced GI Joe in the first place, and were obliged once again to pick up the baton worldwide – so in 1982 they introduced the 'GI Joe: A Real American Hero' range in the USA, and this 3-inch member of the new 'GI Joe Team' (smaller figures were *de rigeur* by now) did battle with mortal enemy 'Cobra Command'.

The new toy line was supported by publications from Marvel Comics, as well as an animated television series. Indeed, it was Marvel Comics who had come up with the 'Cobra' concept in the first place, but initially Hasbro was reluctant to make toys of villains for fear they would not sell. Such fears were ill-founded, however, as baddies amounted to some 40 per cent of the series' sales volume.

In Britain, the new, smaller GI Joe figures also changed name, becoming 'Action Force', while the stateside 'Cobra' antagonists became the 'Red Shadows'. Essentially a terrorist organization, this band of miscreants was led by Baron Ironblood, an evil genius whose 'twisted criminal brain dreams of only one thing … world domination.' Ironblood's right-hand man was the evil Black Major. In the UK, fans of the Red Shadows could follow the exploits of this malevolent bunch on the pages of Battle Action Force comic.

Nick Millen: A Personal Recollection

A friend and work colleague of mine, Nick Millen, fondly remembers the time when the smaller action figures walked tall. Nick recalled:

> One of the most interesting GI Joe/ 'Action Force' figures was a chap called 'Zartan'. In the cartoon he could change his face to impersonate others, so for the action figure they gave him a little backpack that contained a rubberized mask. You would pop the mask on to 'impersonate' somebody, which was really cool.

According to published online GI Joe fanzines, not only could 'Zartan' change his skin colour to blend into whatever environment he found himself in, he was also a master of some twenty languages, an acrobat, a contortionist and even a ventriloquist – 'Action Force''s polymath no less. But back to Nick:

> The other feature the figurine had was the ability to change colour in direct sunlight. He would go a sort of greeny-mauve colour, and the stronger the sunlight was, the darker he became, sort of like the Transformers figures' heat reactive emblems you could breathe on to and rub.

During the second year of the franchise, all Transformers featured what were called 'rubsigns', which revealed either 'Autobot' or 'Decepticon' insignia. Great fun, but the real purpose of this development was to distinguish between authentic Transformers and the increasing number of knock-offs attempting to jump on the toy's band wagon. Nick continued:

> Oddly 'Zartan' also had a removable breastplate that would block the sun and make his chest a normal skin colour, whilst the rest of him went a combination of green and mauve. I've no idea why he possessed this feature.

Thinking back to his school days, when 'Action Force' figures were an exchangeable playground currency,

ABOVE: **'Cobra' was the nemesis of the 'GI Joe Team', and the 'Python Patrol' was an élite unit within it. This 'GI Joe Python Patrol' figure was released by Hasbro for the 25th anniversary in 2008.**

LEFT: **Gracing the pages of the British Battle Action Force comic books, the 'Red Shadows' were fanatically loyal to 'Baron Ironblood'. Palitoy introduced the 'Action Force Red Shadows' in 1983.**

Nick smiled as he recalled another incident from this halcyon period.

At one point during my school days when 'Action Force' was at its peak, one of the kids had been to the USA on holiday and brought a figure into school which his dad bought him out there, but he wasn't into 'Action Force' as much as I was. It was a figure called 'Beach Head' which wasn't even released in the UK at that time – a cool, balaclava-clad military

type – so I set about a plan to offload one of my own 'Action Force' figures known as 'Lifeline' and see if I could get hold of it. 'Lifeline' was a first aid-cum-medic sort of character who had an attachable safety mask and a giant medical bag. He was rubbish.

For the record, 'Lifeline' was the GI Joe Team's rescue trooper, and made its debut in 1986. Dressed in striking red overalls and bright white boots, I'm sure some 'Action Force' fans loved him. Nick continued:

I spent a few lunchtimes going on about how great 'Lifeline' was and that people had repeatedly asked me to trade it for 'Ace', the 'Skystriker''s pilot (they hadn't) which I really didn't care for (I did). I casually said I thought 'Beach Head' looked OK if he wanted to trade it with me. He finally did, and I offloaded my rubbish 'Lifeline' figure for the unreleased and rare 'Beach Head'. I don't remember the child's name, but I do think about it from time to time, and think how he must have been kicking himself a few days later.

I'm sure this story will resonate with other enthusiasts who are familiar with the dog-eat-dog world of collecting and the requisite cunning – or should that be 'ingenuity' – involved in assembling a winning accumulation.

Action Man to the Present Day

GI Joe and Action Man resurrected

Between 1993 and 2006, Hasbro resurrected both the larger GI Joe and Action Man. No longer a fighting man, he was a new man, an action figure modi-

Mego wasn't about to be sidelined during the revolution in smaller action figures, and in 1981 released this 'Eagle Force Kayo the Judo Fighter' figure. A cartoon strip printed on the reverse of the card read: 'Kayo is searching Baron von Chill's warehouse for an illegal weapon shipment when he is jumped by R.I.O.T. troops.' Unusually, this figure was manufactured in diecast metal.

'It's the biggest news since toy soldiers – superbly detailed 7-inch military action figures complete with removable uniforms and equipment. Look out for Battle Brigade in the shops now. You'll want to collect them all.'

fied to suit a new audience. He was now an all-action hero, an athlete who participated in any amount of Xtreme sports. The 'Action Man Skydiver' became the Toy Retailers' Association Boys Toy of the Year in 1997. The new, all-action Action Man now faced adversaries quite different from the bestselling German 'Stormtrooper' he had previously repeatedly encountered. Now he was pitched against 'Dr X', 'No-Face' and the evil 'Professor Gangrene'.

The traditional military figure did make one comeback during this period however, when in 1996 Hasbro released a 30th Anniversary limited edition 12-inch collectors' figure (Palitoy was acquired by Hasbro in 1991).

Though much in the style of the original 1966 'Action Soldier', the new figure differed in proportion to the original. Allegedly the original mould tools were no longer available, so though quite a good match, the new figure was somewhat larger, with bigger hands and a beefier physique. His uniform and accessories were identical however, and the new figure provided many boys of a particular age with a welcome reprise of childhood innocence.

In 1971 Palitoy created its Bradgate division in order to import foreign product and repackaging and rebranding it before selling it on to wholesalers rather than directly to retail outlets, as was its practice with Action Man and its other established toys and games. This mint 1970s vintage 'Little Big Man Tropical Combat' figure was based on an original figure manufactured by Spain's Madelman, who produced similar figures from 1968 until 1983.

Alan Hall's Mission

Then, in 2006, that saviour of our childhood memories, Alan Hall, of UK retailer Modellers Loft, gained a licence from Hasbro to reproduce much of Palitoy's original output. Accomplishing this mission required Mr Hall to destroy much of his own collection of rare vintage packaging, which had to be dismantled and flattened to facilitate duplication. Because it was not obvious from the facsimile packaging that these releases were not original, or that the items inside the

initial wave of the 40th Anniversary Nostalgic Collection were also reproductions, many in the collecting community who had invested a lot of money in authentic items were somewhat annoyed as it was almost impossible to tell the difference between a forty-year-old item and a twenty-first-century copy. Any confusion was remedied in subsequent releases, which were clearly marked '© Hasbro 2006'.

More recently, Art & Science International (A&S) managed to gain a licence from Hasbro to celebrate Action Man's fiftieth birthday by launching a new official range in the UK.

On Thursday 2 November 2017 a green plaque was installed at Palitoy's old toy factory in Jackson Street, Coalville, where the company manufactured some of the most popular toys in Britain between 1937 and 1985. Councillor Pam Posnett from Leicestershire County Council said: 'Palitoy not only helped to stoke children's imaginations with its classic toys and

Palitoy 'Bradgate Little Big Man Pony Express' on horseback. Based on another Madelman original, this close-up provides a good idea of the stunning detail exhibited by these 7-inch giants.

figures, it also helped to put Coalville on the map. It is fantastic to see that eighty years on, there is still huge support from the people of Leicestershire.'

Action Man in 2018

The Action Man story doesn't finish here. More recently, in March 2018, the 'Movable Fighting Man' appeared in an advert for Moneysupermar-ket.com, the British price comparison website. That same month, in its UK Top Shazamed Ads feature, The Drum global media platform declared: 'Action Man boogies on into this week's chart.' The Drum's 'Shazam' chart is based on the number of times each advertisement has been 'shazamed' over the past week using the music identification app.

The Drum's feature went on to explain:

> Moneysupermarket has landed into the chart this week in seventh place with Hasbro's Action Man dancing in the desert... [the clip] starts out with Action Man radioing colleagues in the middle of a warzone to tell them that he just saved on Money-supermarket and now feels epic.

Created by London agency Mother, Moneysuper-market's advertisement featured ingeniously choreo-graphed stop-motion animation showing Action Man strutting through the desert with a back-up troop of dancers, all to the accompaniment of American musi-cian CeCe Peniston's 1991 smash hit *Finally*.

I found the advertisement hilarious, I suspect like the majority of those who saw it, and it was nice to see a classic toy from my past thrust to centre stage again. However, not everyone enjoyed it, and many Action Man enthusiasts were appalled by the mini-ature's admittedly 'camp' antics, arguing that such a frivolous treatment somehow sullied Action Man's memory. Horses for courses I guess, but let's remem-ber, it was only ever... a toy.

This badge dates from 1996, the time when Mattel tried to buy Hasbro in what Peter Allen, who worked for Hasbro then, remembers as their 'surprise' attempt. Said Peter: 'It was commissioned by the packaging studio manager. We arrived at the office to find it on our desks, on the day when our chairman Alan Hassenfeld had a video link call to the office telling us the attempted take-over was a total surprise and would be fully resisted. Alan told us his first knowledge of the bid was a telephone call from the head of Mattel telling him the bid had been launched.' Peter told me that only a very few badges would have been produced, reflecting, 'The question is, how many have survived?'

DRAGON MODELS

Hong Kong-based Dragon Models Limited (Dragon, or DML) was established in 1987 as a sister company to model retailer Universal Models (UML), and benefited from the existing distribution agreement UML enjoyed with leading international model and hobby firms such as Revell/Monogram, Italeri and Hasegawa. After initially concentrating on 1:35-scale plastic kits of military vehicles, Dragon quickly achieved a reputation for excellence amongst enthusiasts.

For action-figure enthusiasts it is the introduction in 1999 of Dragon's 1:6-scale 'New Generation' action-figure series that really set them apart. At last, baby boomers facing middle age could rekindle the joy of playing with Action Man. Dragon's new figures were not toys, of course, but serious collectables! DML's first figure, 'Hans', a German NCO during Operation *Barbarossa* in 1941, set new standards for the 1:6-scale action figure, and made Action Man and GI Joe look frankly childish. For a while DML also produced smaller 1:16-scale military figures – the 'Warrior' series.

Remarkably, Dragon's 1:6-scale action-figure series now stands at over 400 figures, each fully posable and complete with fabulously detailed accessories and fabric uniforms. Subjects range from 'World War II', 'Modern Special Operations' and 'Law Enforcement', to licensed character figures from movies, sports, electronic games and comics.

During the early 2000s, Dragon Models produced hundreds of action figures, most of them being World War II German figures. However, after 2010, the number of figures that it produced began to decline sharply, and it stopped producing 1:6-scale action figures in November 2012.

Dragon 'World War II Austria 1945 LAH Division Private (Schutze) Alfred' (1999).

Dragon naked do-it-yourself action figure and accessory sets.

GILBERT AND MEGO EMBRACE THE FILM AND TELEVISION MERCHANDIZING BONANZA

The late Bernard Loomis is credited with the first use of the word 'toyetic', which he employed whilst discussing the opportunities for producing figures for *Close Encounters of the Third Kind* with the movie's creator, Steven Spielberg. Back then, Loomis worked for US toy giant Kenner. An American toy developer and marketer, Loomis was the promotional driving force behind the success of such brands as 'Chatty Cathy', Barbie, Hot Wheels and 'Strawberry Short-cake', but is perhaps best known for his efforts behind the success of *Star Wars*' toy merchandise.

Now widely used, 'toyetic' refers to the suitability of a movie or other media property for toy merchandizing. Loomis appeared to have had the golden touch, and in his time worked for Mattel, General Mills and Hasbro; during his tenure at each of these companies they were successively able to claim the position of 'the world's largest toy company'.

Films and Toy Merchandizing

Today such 'tie-in' licences are a very important part of the revenue stream for any major new release, and licence deals for books, computer games, magazines, apparel merchandizing (garments such as T-shirts)

and toys, of course, are highly sought after. But as we have seen, this wasn't always the case, and until Loomis leveraged the merchandizing agreement George Lucas had brokered with Twentieth Century Fox, the studios weren't too bothered about things they considered peripheral to the prime objective: healthy box-office receipts.

The 007 Franchise

As far as action figures are concerned, the 007 franchise was probably the first property that revealed just what could be achieved with toy merchandizing. Three companies, two of the them American, Mego and Gilbert, and a now little-known British one, Cecil Coleman, produced a range of Bond-themed action figures which have since become very collectable. Mego's astronaut-outfitted James Bond from *Moon-raker*, and Cecil Coleman 12-inch figures from *You Only Live Twice* are especially sought after today by collectors.

Because of 007's vast array of weapons and gadgets, an enormous variety of licensed toys were produced. Leading the pack were 'Lone Star', whose James Bond '007 *Thunderball* Ricochet Gun' is amongst the holy grail of James Bond collectables. Perhaps the most successful 007 toy ever was Corgi's diecast 'Aston Martin DB5', released at the same time as *Goldfinger* hit cinema screens in 1964. Featuring a working ejector seat so Bond could expel the gun-wielding passenger sitting next to him, a pop-up armoured shield, machine guns and extending tyre shredders, this toy was peerless.

British kit manufacturer Airfix released scale replicas of the DB5 as well as the Toyota 2000 GT from the 1967 movie *You Only Live Twice*, and A. C. Gilbert made good use of their licence, which covered not just action figures but a wide variety of accessory sets, such as attaché cases stuffed with gadgets and concealed weapons.

Currently the more than two dozen Bond movies have grossed nearly $7 billion: it is therefore no wonder that owners EON Productions Limited see no need to bring the franchise to an end.

Star Wars and the True Value of Tie-In Merchandise

To start with, toy manufacturers were cautious, and waited to see if a movie was going to explode or be a dud before they committed to the expensive tool-

Gilbert figure of Sean Connery as James Bond from 1965's blockbuster *Thunderball*.

Gilbert mint-on-card M's desk set and 007's attaché case (1965).

ing, production and packaging costs for an associated range of toy merchandise. That is, until *Star Wars* broke the mould and revealed the true value of tie-in merchandise, the space saga remarkably earning twice as much revenue for its toys as its box office receipts.

Even so, whilst researching one of my books about the international plastic kit industry, I had the pleasure of staying at the Chicago home of a senior executive for US kit giant Revell-Monogram, and he explained how risky it was to agree to

movie licences – something that Revell-Monogram did more than most. He told me that such licences were especially risky because the deal for them was dependent on kit companies agreeing to a fee they were obliged to pay *up front*, and which was calculated on an estimate of the number of kits they hoped to shift. This amount was paid even if their calculations proved wildly ambitious. If the movie was a failure, manufacturers were both out of pocket and left with a great deal of unwanted inventory.

Original Hong Kong-made Mego 'Klingon' figure (1974).

DENYS FISHER

The late Denys Fisher is an English engineer most famous for inventing the spirograph drawing toy in the 1960s, which he originally fashioned from a variety of Meccano construction toy components. Initially on sale in Leeds in 1965, Spirograph went on to secure sixteen patents and worldwide sales, being licensed to Kenner in the US and becoming UK Toy of the Year in 1967. Denys Fisher Toys went on to produce a range of other toys and board games, and was sold to Palitoy in 1970. It was subsequently acquired by Hasbro. Through the 1980s and 1990s, Fisher continued to work with Hasbro, developing new toys and further refining Spirograph. As far as action figures are concerned, the Denys Fisher brand is probably most famous for its enormously successful 'Six Million Dollar Man' and Bionic Woman ranges.

Denys Fisher 'The Six Million Dollar Man' (1974).

Multi-Episode Television Series and Toy Merchandizing

Because movies are sometimes one-hit wonders, standalone productions that often do not benefit from the effect of sequels to build brand loyalty, toy manufacturers have traditionally preferred to ally themselves to multi-episode television series, which, because of their repetitive nature, are more likely to encourage recall and steadily develop a following.

Consequently, in the 1970s, successful television series such as *Star Trek*, *The Six Million Dollar Man*, *The A-Team* and *The Dukes of Hazard* appeared much safer bets than a new movie. And anyway, because of their regular presence in weekly schedules, episodes from television series quickly developed a loyal fan base. At a time when the law restricted the opportunities for toy brands to exploit the value of their alliances with programme makers by advertising directly at children, instead they had to rely on the ubiquity of

what youngsters had seen on television to generate 'pester power' and the 'nag factor', as the phenomena are known in the USA.

Marketing Past and Present

Although children are becoming one of the most targeted groups for advertisers and marketers, legal regulation still restricts how publicists can address this sector. In Norway, for example, advertisers are forbidden to single out children under twelve years of age at all, whilst in the USA what legal restrictions exist are subject to self-regulation by the media itself and are consequently less severe.

The European Union's Audiovisual Media Services Directive, which came into force in 2009, stipulates that advertisers must not directly encourage minors to persuade their parents or others to purchase the

goods or services being advertised, and that product placement is forbidden in children's programmes. Similarly, between 1946 and 1983, legislation in the USA limited the scope for advertisers to target children. The Children's Television Acts of 1990 and 1996 also went some way to tightening things up.

TOP LEFT: **Mego 'Fonzie' from Happy Days (1976): his hands could be manipulated to reveal his typical thumbs-up pose. *'Ayyy!'***

TOP RIGHT: **Mego 'Hutch' figure from *Starsky & Hutch* mint-in-blister pack (1976).**

LEFT: **1977's *Saturday Night Fever* had propelled John Travolta into the celebrity stratosphere, so it is no surprise that the same year American manufacturer Chemtoy released a figure of him. 'The industry's most complete, most versatile line of fast-selling, profitable low-end toys.' Chemtoy manufactured what the USA calls 'Rack Toys' – the cheaper, more colourful carded toys hanging from rotating carousel displays in dime stores, 7-Elevens and pharmacies.**

BANDAI

Tokyo-based Bandai can trace its genesis back to the immediate post-war years when Naoharu Yamashina was working for his brother-in-law, a textile wholesaler. This sector was in decline, however, and Yamashina persuaded his relative that the toy industry was where the real money was, and encouraged him to invest in it. In 1950, Yamashina took full control of the toy distribution business, renaming it Bandai-ya, which was shortened to Bandai in 1961.

The company grew rapidly, and in 1958 even boasted its own television campaign.

Bandai launched its famous 'Astro Boy' toy in 1963. Based on the character from the popular manga and animé series, this heralded a new business opportunity for the company, and over the following decades, Bandai manufactured toys with ties to the 'Kamen Rider' television character, the 'Space Battleship Yamato' programme, 'Ultraman', the 'Power Rangers' and the 'Gundam' series.

Bandai continued to expand in the 1970s with the creation of several sub-sidiaries; a joint-venture Tonka Japan in 1970, and the hugely popular Bandai Models in 1971, their 1/48-scale AFV models dominating that segment of the model kit market.

Bandai 'Terrahawks Hawkwing' and 'Space Sergeant' 101 (1983).

Founder Naoharu Yamashina revolutionized the structure of Bandai, and in May 1980 his son Makoto became president. The same year, Bandai also launched the iconic 'Gundam Plastic Models' based on an existing hit animated series, and in November 1985 introduced the first video game based on the manga *Kinnikuman*, selling more than one million copies.

Today, Bandai is Japan's leading toy company, and holds the licences to such enormously popular action-figure phenomena as 'Daikaiju', 'Ultraman', 'Super Robot', 'Kamen Rider', the 'Super Sentai' and 'Power Rangers' series (which they helped to originate), 'Gundam' and many others.

Bandai 'New Captain Scarlet' and 'Destiny Angel' action figures (2004).

The Toy Trade Press

To assist toy manufacturers and retailers navigate these often-treacherous waters and optimize their marketing effort towards this most promising constituency, from the late nineteenth century, on both sides of the Atlantic, a toy trade press has existed. In March 1891, the *Toy Trades Journal* was first published, to be followed by *Playthings* magazine in 1902, *Sports Trader* in 1907 and the *Games, Toys and Amusements Journal* in 1908. Post-war, just before the television revolution changed the landscape forever, children's comic books and magazines proved the most lucrative media for toy brands to communicate their wares.

Televised Toy Commercials

In 1955, the first televised toy commercial, broadcast, as you might imagine, in the United States, was for Hasbro's bestselling 'Mr Potato Head', a toy that would be knocked off its pedestal with the advent of Barbie in 1959. Interestingly, it was because of the relaxed rules regarding product placement in the USA that John Lasseter's 1995 movie, *Toy Story*, reversed the declining sales of 'Mr Potato Head', 'Slinky Dog' and 'Etch A Sketch' and reinvigorated these vintage toys, all of which had featured alongside 'Buzz' and 'Woody'.

Regulations governing what could and could not be advertised to children worldwide on television, and the considerable cost of such media at a time when, in Britain for example, there was only one commercial channel and no competition from any other audio-visual media, meant that even in the 1960s and 70s, internationally children's comics offered one of the best-value platforms for toy advertisements.

CEJI

Headquartered in Drancy, in the north-eastern suburbs of Paris, the Compagnie Générale du Jouet was founded in 1969. Its main factories were located at Illkirch-Graffenstaden in Alsace, and Champagnole in eastern France. In Hong Kong, outsourced mould production, printing and packaging also took place. A Ceji subsidiary in the USA and a sourcing office in China dealt with licences for foreign markets.

Joustra, a subsidiary of Ceji, held the licence to market Takara's transforming 'Diaclone' (strong as a diamond, fast as a cyclone) toys in France, Belgium, the Netherlands and Germany, but in 1985 Hasbro introduced the 'Transformers' brand to continental Europe via their own subsidiary, Milton Bradley (MB), effectively monopolizing the territories where Joustra had previously held the 'Diaclone' licence. Although Joustra continued to sell toys under the 'Diaclone' brand, Takara was more focused on producing Transformers-branded toys for the North American market, and as a result, some toys with factory-applied 'Autobot' or 'Decepticon' stickers were sold in Joustra 'Diaclone' packaging.

When Joustra's parent company, Ceji, succumbed to financial trouble in 1985, the upshot was that Hasbro/MB acquired the existing 'Diaclone' stock and encouraged Joustra to put these toys into newly created Transformers packaging. This arrangement resulted in several anomalies, such as the second wave of Joustra 'Diaclone' toys becoming much rarer than the first, and also explains why 'Optimus Prime' was originally absent from the MB line-up, as any toy released by Joustra was off limits to MB due to Joustra's exclusive contract with Takara until the Joustra/MB deal was up and running. This is why the MB version of 'Tracks' (the transforming Corvette) is red, the toy's original 'Diaclone' colour, instead of blue in line with 'Tranformers' convention, and why 'Thundercracker' was sold in 'Starscream' packaging with 'Starscream''s sticker sheet. During this period Ceji continued to manufacture toys for Hasbro/MB, such as the 'Insecticons' and some 'Constructicons'.

Sadly, Ceji's worsening financial troubles meant that by the end of 1985 the business was wound up.

Denys Fisher 'Angels nurses' from the BBC television series about student nurses at the fictitious St Angela's hospital (1977).

All this would change of course, firstly when VCRs gave viewers the ability to choose what and when they would watch on television, skipping advertisement breaks as desired, and later, when the plethora of new cable and satellite channels broke the long-enjoyed monopoly of traditional commercial broadcasters – and finally, when the internet challenged the viability of all traditional advertising media. Until then, comics such as *Eagle*, *Victor*, *Valiant*, *Warlord*, *Action* and *TV 21* (which ultimately merged with *Valiant*) were the best places to promote toys such as action figures.

A New Era for Action Figures

All this changed in 1983, when federal regulations in the USA prohibiting the creation of children's TV programming based on toys were lifted. This heralded a new era for action figures. In 1981, Mattel were one of the first companies to take advantage of the relaxation in the rules when they created a cartoon

series based on their 'He-Man' and the 'Masters of the Universe' action figures. So successful was this synergy that Mattel sold over 55 million units that year, and up until 1990, a total of over $1 billion in revenue was generated.

Of all the companies that elevated licensed toys to new heights, two stand out. The first is Amercan company A. C. Gilbert – it is now largely forgotten, but during its heyday it towered head and shoulders above its rivals. The other is Mego, also no longer with us but still well known amongst collectors.

The A. C. Gilbert Company

At its height A. C. Gilbert was one of the largest toy companies in the world. Because of the similarities between its metal 'Erector' construction set and Frank Hornby's famous product, many enthusiasts still know it as the 'American Meccano', despite the fact that both inventions were noticeably different, and both were developed independently of each other.

A. C. GILBERT

Alfred Carlton Gilbert was originally a magician, and in 1909 he incorporated the Mysto Manufacturing Company, specializing in magicians' sets: established in Westville, Connecticut, the business was originally to provide supplies for magic shows, a field he naturally knew well. However, Gilbert's invention of the 'Erector' construction toy in 1911, allegedly inspired by railroad girders, but no doubt also influenced by the success of Frank Hornby's Meccano, was the company's first real breakthrough. In 1916 the firm's name was therefore changed to the A. C. Gilbert Company. In 1929, Gilbert bought the US company producing Meccano, and it continued production as American Meccano until 1938.

As it gradually moved away from merchandise for magicians, the company diversified, and in 1922 started with another very successful line: chemistry sets. By the 1950s A. C. Gilbert was riding along with the atomic zeitgeist – the company even released a set that featured a Geiger counter as a supplement to the numerous Duck & Cover drills American youngsters were obliged to endure at school.

In 1938 Gilbert had purchased 'American Flyer', a struggling manufacturer of toy trains. A. C. Gilbert redesigned the entire product line and introduced a selection of HO-scale trains under the brand name Gilbert HO. During World War II, A. C. Gilbert produced equipment

Rare carded Gilbert James Bond assortment (1965).

Alfred Carlton Gilbert's first love was magic, and in 1909, together with his friend John Petrie, he founded the Mysto Manufacturing Company. Created to provide 'Mysto Magic' products to magicians and entertainers in magic shows, the firm's range soon expanded to provide magic sets available to everyone, from novices in their teens to adult professionals.

The World of Construction Toys

The 'Erector Structural Steel Builder' was Mysto's next creation, launched at the New York City Toy Fair in 1911. It was a departure for the company and definitely something off the beaten track. Developed by Gilbert and his wife Mary, 'Erector' was inspired by the steel girders then used prominently in the construction of the new urban railways, for bridges and other structures. Despite its novelty, this departure into the world of construction toys proved a great success. In 1916, the name of the company was changed to the A. C. Gilbert Company.

True to form, for the next few decades A. C. Gilbert involved itself in a variety of seemingly disconnected ventures, everything from regenerative vacuum-tube radio receivers (radios) to running Connecticut's station WCJ, and the manufacture of chemistry sets

Gilbert James Bond toy-shop shelf talker.

for military aircraft, but when the conflict ended the company returned to the production of toys.

In 1965, A. C. Gilbert produced James Bond movie tie-in figures, and a slot-car road-race set featuring Bond's Aston Martin DB5. This licence proved an enormous success, and the company's 007 products from this period are amongst some of the most highly sought-after toy collectables.

The company was the largest employer in New Haven, the coastal city that was its base – which, incidentally, can claim to be the first planned city in the USA after English Puritans laid out the street scheme as far back as 1638. From the early 1930s through to the late 1950s, A. C. Gilbert's Sound Street Manufacturing facility in Connecticut employed more than 5,000 people in three shifts, operating round the clock.

The death of its founder in 1961 naturally caused shock waves, and the Gilbert family divested itself of ownership. By the end of the 1960s the company was failing to make a profit, and in 1967 effectively disappeared after the Erector brand was sold to Gabriel Industries and American Flyer was acquired by Lionel.

– even one featuring a Geiger counter and radioactive samples. In 1929, Gilbert bought the US licence holder of Hornby's Meccano, thereby deservedly holding the 'American Meccano' epithet until just before the outbreak of World War II.

From 1934, 'Gilbert Microscope Outfits' proved another successful line for the company.

New Fields for A. C. Gilbert

In 1938, Gilbert's purchase of American Flyer, a failing manufacturer of toy trains, marked its entry into another new field. The advent of the Cold War, and especially the space race, triggered in 1957 by the appearance of Sputnik, encouraged Gilbert to produce affordable telescopes and an accompanying comic book, *Adventures in Science*, in which the enigmatic Mr Science guided a previously disinterested teenage boy on a journey through time and space in an effort to rekindle his interest in science.

Physics was replaced by Hollywood in the mid-1960s when A. C. Gilbert secured a licence to produce James Bond toy merchandise with a series of character figures and slot cars, including Bond's iconic Aston Martin DB5.

The death of A. C. Gilbert in 1961 persuaded family members to sell their shares, and progressively the

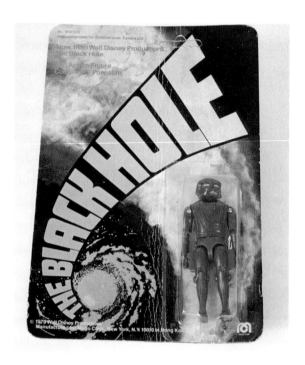

'Sentry Robot' from Walt Disney's *The Black Hole*. Mego (1979).

LEFT: **Mego 'John Boy' and 'Ellen' from television's** *The Waltons* (1978).

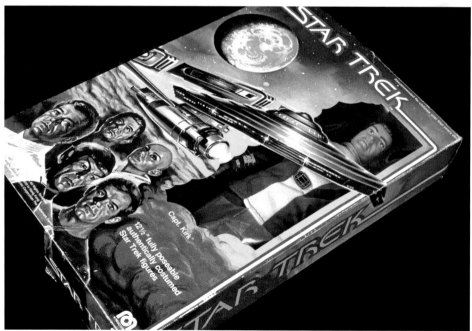

1979 vintage Mego 'Captain Kirk' from *Star Trek: The Motion Picture* exhibiting Mego's propensity for the faces of their figures to lose colour.

company's fortunes declined; the company was never profitable under its new ownership.

By 1967, Gilbert had finally gone out of business, with its famous Erector brand sold to Gabriel Industries who marketed the product with the catch phrase, *The construction toy from A. C. Gilbert*, emblazoned on their packaging. Lionel, the US equivalent of Hornby Railways, purchased American Flyer from Gilbert and also pinched a slogan from them, in this instance adding the well-established *Developed at the Gilbert Hall of Science*, to their product boxes.

A. C. Gilbert are sure to be principally remembered for their 'Erector' and 'American Flyer' ranges, but in the context of this book their action-figure releases are up there with the best.

Espionage Blockbuster Series

Gilbert enjoyed a long association with EON Productions' 007 franchise, releasing a successful series of 3-inch figures inspired by the first Bond movies, *Dr No* and *Thunderball*. This carded, blister-packed series featured a full range of characters, goodies and baddies; alongside representations of 007 himself in a variety of dinner jackets, tuxedos and wet suits (complete with aqualung and spear gun), there were miniatures of the evil Dr No and his lethal bowler hat-wielding accomplice Oddjob. So successful were the 3-inch figures, it was inevitable that Gilbert followed them up with much larger, boxed 12-inch versions, all of which are now very rare and eminently collectable.

Interestingly, James Bond creator Ian Fleming was involved in the concept stage of another very successful espionage blockbuster series: *Man from U.N.C.L.E.* This MGM television series told the story of the ongoing contests between the multi-national United Network Command for Law and Enforcement and its nemesis, the evil THRUSH (Technological Hierarchy for the Removal of Undesirables and Subjugation of Humanity) syndicate. Every inch the US James Bond, Napoleon Solo, played by actor Robert Vaughn, and his suave Russian sidekick, Illya Kuryakin (David McCallum) got in and out of numerous tights spots, often with the help of a bevy of gadgets and special

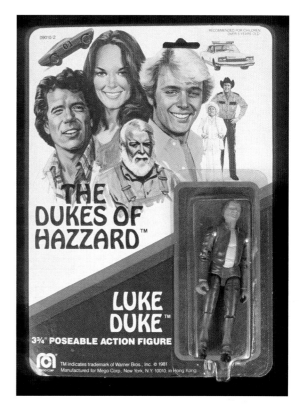

'Mego Luke Duke' action figure from *The Dukes of Hazzard* mint-in-blister pack (1981).

weapons, making them ideal subjects for accessory-wielding action figures.

All manufacturers of action figures attempt to get the maximum out of existing mould tools, and A. C. Gilbert were no exception. Accordingly, their two *Man from U.N.C.L.E.* 12-inch figures of Solo and Kuryakin featured the same spring-release arm mechanism previously installed in Gilbert's 'James Bond' and 'Oddjob' figures. Dressed in black trousers and white shirt, and armed with a cap-firing pistol, Solo was suave and deadly. Kuryakin also came equipped with a cap-firing pistol but was dressed rather more casually, wearing black turtle-neck sweater and trousers. Each figure also came with a plastic U.N.C.L.E ID badge, and today, surviving figures complete with this accessory are now very rare. The boxed figures came complete with a wide variety of accessories including a neat box of 'bee roll caps' (repeating paper caps) for the agents' pistols, which also came with shoulder stocks, telescopic sights and barrel extensions, which turned these handguns into sniper rifles.

Crime Drama Television Series *Honey West*

Honey West was an American crime drama television series that aired during the 1965–1966 television season. The television series starred Anne Francis as female private detective Honey West. Although she played the first female detective on television, Anne

Francis wasn't entirely new to audiences, having featured in the hit sci-fi movie *Forbidden Planet* in 1956.

Intended as the USA's counterpart to Cathy Gale and Emma Peel, John Steed's sexy female confederates in the British television series *The Avengers*, Honey West capitalized on her female charms, and Gilbert's action figure of her made the most of her allure, equipment sets for the figure sporting the legend 'Accessories for TV's Private Eye-Full'. The third action-figure licence that A. C. Gilbert acquired in the sixties, 'Honey West' could be dressed in skin-tight

Mattel 1982 vintage 'He-Man' figure from the *Masters of the Universe* franchise.

leotard and black boots, and with her gold belt, holster and pistol, the sexist soubriquet did seem appropriate.

Mint-in-box examples of vintage 'Honey West' figures, especially those complete with Honey's pet ocelot, the mini leopard of the Americas, are worth a small fortune. The accessory sets are somewhat easier to find. There was a 'Karate Outfit', a 'Formal Outfit' and a 'Secret Agent Outfit', which contained everything the best-dressed lady spy needs. There was even a carded set featuring a spare ocelot for those who had lost the one that came with the boxed figure. This version of Honey's pet featured a movable head and legs, and came complete with a lead attached to a pearl collar. This set even featured a pair of binoculars with real lenses.

Despite airing for only one series, *Honey West* was well received by critics, and Anne Francis won a Golden Globe for her efforts.

Gilbert's output wasn't all spies and gadgets. Embracing the zeitgeist of the space race they also put their own man into the cosmos – but there is much more about spaceman Moon McDare in Chapter 4.

TOP: **He-Man minicomic: 'Skeletor's Dragon'.**

BOTTOM: **'Major Margaret "Hot Lips" Houlihan' from *M.A.S.H. Tristar International (1982).***

MEGO

Founded in 1954 by D. David and Madeline Abrams, throughout the 1950s and 1960s Mego did good business selling cheap 'dime store' toy imports. Then in 1971, the Abrams' son Martin, a business-school graduate, decided the company should be an initiator and began to move Mego towards the action-figures field. Employing a model based on using generic bodies but relying on interchangeable outfits to provide variety, he kept costs to the minimum. Consequently, Mego figures proved both popular and inexpensive. Another saving was the fact that Mego primarily adopted an 8-inch scale for their figures – where GI Joe stood 12 inches tall – and relied on manufacturing in the British Crown Colony of Hong

Mego 'Tom Baker' from *Dr Who* manufactured by Harbert in Spain (1979).

Mego 'Fonzie' from *Happy Days* (1976).

Kong, from whence some 60 per cent of their products were imported.

One of Mego's first toys under Martin Adams was an original character, 'Action Jackson', meant to compete with Hasbro's popular GI Joe line. Heavily promoted on television commercials and in newspaper advertisements, the 'Action Jackson' line was a big seller on its 1971 launch, but soon faded; it was discontinued after 1974.

In 1972 Mego secured the licences to create toys for both National Periodical Publications (DC Comics) and Marvel Comics, and until these rights lapsed, Mego's 'The World's Greatest Super Heroes' series of 8-inch figures established a new standard for the 1970s. Another Mego first was the introduction of fully clothed figures packaged in carded blister packs; this was brought about because retailers simply didn't have the shelf space to stock action figures in traditional boxes, but wanted to display them on peg boards or hanging from carousels.

Other licences followed, and tie-ins with *The Flint-stones, Happy Days, Laverne & Shirley, Our Gang, Star-sky & Hutch, The Waltons, Wizard of Oz, Wonder Woman* and 1978's *Superman* movie, kept Mego on the up and up, their figures of Superman, 'Jor-El', 'Lex Luthor' and 'General Zod' proving particularly popular.

From 1976, Mego produced a small collection of World War II-themed military action figures; these were marketed internationally under the Lion Rock brand, and in the USA under the 'Johnny Action' or 'Combat Man' brand name. Intended to compete with Spain's Madel-man line of soldier figures, this new range proved surpris-ingly unsuccessful.

Mego's 'Eagle Force' comprised a range of 70mm diecast action figures and was a counter-terrorist task force, like Hasbro's 'G.I. Joe: A Real American Hero' action figures.

Mego extended its licences into the world of film merchandizing, negotiating terms with major studios and television companies, which led to a range of figures associated with properties including *Planet of the Apes, Star Trek* and *Tarzan*.

1976 was a busy year, as Martin Abrams also signed an agreement with Japanese toy manufacturer Takara to bring their popular 'Microman' figures to the United States under the name 'Micronauts'. However, he turned down the opportunity to license toys for the upcoming motion picture *Star Wars*, competitor Kenner Products obtaining Geoge Lucas's extremely profitable enterprise instead.

Realizing that sci-fi would be the competitive genre, Mego quickly secured licences for *Buck Rogers in the 25th Century, The Black Hole* and *Star Trek: The Motion Picture*. Future success appeared guaranteed; during the early 1980s Mego also produced action figures linked to popular US television shows including *CHiPs, Dallas*, and *Dukes of Hazzard*.

Although of high quality and now very collectable, the trend was towards the smaller and simpler 3-inch figures introduced to support the emerging *Star Wars* franchise. Mego's star was on the wane.

To diversify and perhaps generate new revenue streams, Mego explored the field of electronic toys, but these proved less successful than action figures, and required a tremendous investment. Mego was in trou-ble, and reported losses in 1980 and 1981. In 1982 the company was rocked by financial crisis, filing for Chapter 11 bankruptcy and finally going under in 1983. Neverthe-less, as recently as 2009 Martin Abrams' new company, Abrams Gentile Entertainment (AGE), announced they had regained the rights to the name 'Mego'.

In early 2009 Martin ('Marty) Abrams eventually succeeded in regaining the rights to his family's legacy, and in July 2018 the revived Mego Corporation announced that they were to produce a limited run of their classic-style clothed action figures. At the time of writing, Mego Corp, now called Marty Abrams Presents Mego, has made a significant return to the world of action figures; this, despite the fact that its legendary founder was now well into his seventh decade.

Carded Mego action figure of 'Isaac', the bartender from Aaron Spellings' hit US television series *The Love Boat* (1981).

Galoob large-scale 'Mr T figure' (1983): 'I pity the fool.'

Mego

Another company that was especially adroit at maximizing the full potential from licensing deals was Mego, founded in 1954 by D. David and Madeline Abrams. In the 1950s and early 1960s, before the rising cost of newspaper advertising forced them to change their business model, Mego prospered as an importer of dime store toys. In 1971, the Abrams' son Martin, a recent graduate of business school, was named company president.

Under Martin Abrams' direction, the company shifted its production to dolls with interchangeable bodies: generic bodies could be mass produced, and different figures created by simply interposing different heads and costumes on them. This cost-effective method of production was not only financially prudent, it made practical sense, because in most cases, the only visible body component of a clothed, articulated figure is the head and face.

Early Lines and Figures

Collectors of action figures consider 'Fighting Yank', Mego's answer to Hasbro's GI Joe, to be one of the most sought after. This is not surprising, because in the face of a lawsuit from Hasbro, shortly after Mego introduced the figure in 1964 they were obliged to discontinue production if they were to avoid potentially unlimited costs. Indeed, at the time it was alleged to be so similar that it had, perhaps, been copied directly from authentic GI Joe tooling.

Another early Mego figure is one based on New York Jets quarterback Joe Namath, which is now coveted by collectors. And there is 'Action Jackson', which, like 'Fighting Yank', was also intended as a rival for Hasbro's popular GI Joe line. Heavily promoted on television commercials and in newspaper advertisements, the 'Action Jackson' line, which included figures, vehicles and playsets, was another big seller when it made its debut in 1971; however, it soon

'Apollo Creed' from *Rocky III*, Phoenix Toys (1983).

faded in popularity and was discontinued after 1974. The body design was reused for many of Mego's subsequent 8-inch licensed character action figures. The figures can still be found, but mint-on-card examples of 'Action Jackson' outfits and accessories are now proving particularly hard to locate.

Beginning in 1972, Mego released the first comprehensive line of DC Comics and Marvel Comics superhero and villain figures – 'The World's Greatest Super Heroes!' ('WGSH'). Initially the range included Batman, Robin, Aquaman and Superman figures. The earliest figures were released in a solid box, but these boxes were often damaged by shoppers eager to see the figure inside, so the box design was quickly changed to a window-style box so the contents could be seen, avoiding the situation where potential purchasers needed to open the packaging. The WGSH line was offered from 1972 until 1983.

Fashion Dolls

Mego marketed various fashion doll lines designed to compete with Mattel's Barbie. In 1973 Mego brought the 'Maddie Mod' range to market. This not only included an extensive wardrobe, but also 'Maddie''s boyfriend, 'Richie'. However, 'Maddie Mod' failed to secure enough support from American youngsters,

Carded LJN Paul Atreides action figure (right), and mint in-box 'Sandworm' from David Lynch's movie *Dune* (1984).

so Mego introduced 'Dinah-Mite', a posable, 8-inch scale, Barbie-like doll with a boyfriend named 'Don'. Sadly, 'Dinah-Mite' wasn't much more successful than her predecessor.

Mego's next creations were 'Beautiful Lainie', a large 19-inch doll that danced back and forth from the hips, and 'Candi', a range including 'Coppertone Candi', a tanning doll co-branded with the famous Coppertone sunscreen brand: though not million-sellers, they are still much admired by collectors.

Celebrity Dolls for 1976

In 1976, Mego launched a highly successful 12½-inch celebrity doll range. The first dolls produced were of Sonny and Cher, with costumes designed by American fashion designer Bob Mackie, who, having designed costumes for Diana Ross, Judy Garland and Bette Midler, was at the height of his fame. Mego was famous for their launch parties, and in the mid-seventies the company threw one at the Waldorf-Astoria in Manhattan, where, to a huge invited audience, Sonny and Cher revealed the brand-new dolls of themselves. Later, both dolls were formally unveiled on *The Mike Douglas Show*, the presenter a former big band era singer who now attracted a sizeable afternoon audience. So successful were the Cher figures that they became the top-selling dolls in the USA in 1976, and helped to propel Mego to the position of sixth-ranked domestic toy manufacturer.

Figures Based on Television

The success of figures based on *Planet of the Apes* and *Star Trek* encouraged Mego to explore other television-licensed figures. Soon, using established body parts that simply required the sculpting of new faces, and the production of suitable outfits and packaging, Mego added figures taken from *The Flintstones*, *Happy Days*, *Laverne & Shirley*, *Our Gang*, *Starsky & Hutch*, *The Waltons* and *The Wizard of Oz* to their catalogue.

Mars attacks! 'Martian Spy Girl' by Trendmasters (1996).

In 1977 Mego supplemented their range of television-associated figures with the addition of the 'Lynda Carter Wonder Woman' line, a range that included a figure of 'Wonder Woman' in a factory-painted bustier top with star-spangled bottoms, bracelets, golden lasso, tiara and red boots. The range included 'Nubia', Wonder Woman's super-foe 'Queen Hippolyta', her mother, and 'Major Steve Trevor', her best friend and boss.

In 1978 Mego added figures from the *Superman* movie, including the eponymous superhero 'Jor-El', 'Lex Luthor' and 'General Zod'.

Continuing to exploit this rich seam, in the early 1980s Mego produced figures and vehicles for other successful television shows such as *CHiPs*, *Dallas*, *Dukes of Hazzard* and *The Greatest American Hero*. The *Dukes of Hazzard* figures sold well and were produced

Star Trek: The Next Generation and *Deep Space Nine* characters. *From left to right:* Data the android; Lieutenant Commander Geordi La Forge; Worf the first Klingon main character to appear in the franchise; and Quark, the Ferengi.

BELOW: 'Matrix Trinity' action figure based on the Wachowski brothers' hit 1999 movie. Manufactured by N2 Toys, a company established in 2000 by former Kenner designer Ron Hayes, the *Matrix* figures were his company's debut enterprise. The short-lived N2 Toys went on to make figures associated with *Mad Max*, *Rambo* and the fantasy artist Frank Frazetta. These *Matrix* figures are now highly collectible.

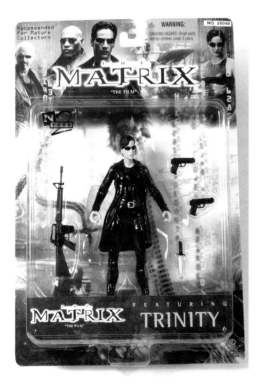

Hasbro 'Captain Leo Davidson', the main protagonist in the 2001 *Planet of the Apes* movie.

COLECO

Founded by Maurice Greenberg in 1932, American company Coleco Industries Inc. began life as 'The Connecticut Leather Company', but by the 1980s had become a highly successful toy company, known for its 'Cabbage Patch Kids' dolls. It was also very successful in the burgeoning video-games sector from that period, and its Coleco Telstar dedicated consoles and ColecoVision video-game consoles proved enormously popular.

Initially the business supplied leather 'shoe findings', the supplies and paraphernalia of a shoe repair shop, but by 1938 the business had started to sell rubber footwear, the demand for which soared after America entered the war in 1941. By the end of the war the company had branched out into new and used shoe machinery, hat-cleaning equipment and shoeshine stands.

By the early 1950s, having diversified further, Coleco was making leather lacing and leathercraft kits. At the New York Toy Fair in 1954, their leather moccasin kit was selected as a Child Guidance Prestige Toy, an achievement that persuaded the Connecticut Leather Company to concentrate wholeheartedly on the toy business.

In 1961 the leather and shoe-findings portion of

Coleco
'Rambo Force
of Freedom'
action figure
(1985)

the business was sold, and Coleco went public. In 1963 it acquired the Kestral Corporation of Springfield, Massachusetts, a manufacturer of inflatable vinyl pools and toys (Coleco had earlier been a pioneer of plastic moulding and the new technique of vacuum forming). Quite soon Coleco had become the largest manufacturer of above-ground swimming pools in the world.

The success of Atari's Pong console encouraged dozens of companies to introduce game systems, and Coleco entered the video-game console business with 'The Telstar' in 1976.

Coleco returned to the video-game console market in 1982 with the launch of 'ColecoVision', but wisely, the company spread the risk of producing bespoke items by introducing a line of ROM cartridges for the Atari 2600 and Intellivision.

As home computers began to challenge the existing video-game business, the Coleco Adam home computer was introduced, but this was unsuccessful and Coleco withdrew from electronics early in 1985.

However, the company had begun to exploit another rich seam, and in 1983 released the 'Cabbage Patch Kids' series of dolls, with huge success. Riding high, in 1986 Coleco went on to purchase Selchow & Righter, manufacturers of the games Scrabble, Parcheesi and Trivial Pursuit. Unfortunately the purchase didn't deliver the promised result and sales of the games plummeted, resulting in warehouses full of unsold games.

Coleco had also recently introduced an ALF plush toy based on the furry alien character with its own television series, as well as producing a talking 'Storytelling' ALF doll. However, the company's investment in Selchow & Righter, the disastrous Adam computer, and the public's dwindling interest in 'Cabbage Patch' dolls, all contrib-

Coleco 'Rambo Weapons Pack' (1985).

uted to Coleco's financial decline, and in 1988 the company filed for bankruptcy.

A restructured Coleco sold off all its American assets, outsourcing work to foreign countries instead. In 1988, Canada-based SLM Action Sports Inc. purchased Coleco's swimming pool and snow goods divisions, and in 1989, Hasbro purchased most of Coleco's remaining product lines.

In 2005, River West Brands, now Chicago-based Dormitus Brands, reintroduced the Coleco brand, and in 2006 the revitalized company introduced the Coleco Sonic, a hand-held game system.

In December 2015, Coleco Holdings announced the development of the 'Coleco Chameleon', a new cartridge-based video-game system, the release of which was scheduled for early 2016; however, because it received poor reviews, Coleco Holdings was encouraged to terminate the project.

in enormous numbers (which is why so many mint-on-card figures can be acquired forty years later), but Mego failed with its *CHiPs* and *Dallas* dolls, and consequently these are much harder to find.

Figures for Sci-Fi Movies

Probably the most famous Mego action figures are the 'Micronauts', produced from 1976 to 1980 under licence from Takara and based on the Japanese company's 'Microman'. So successful were they, that in 1979, Marvel Comics launched a 'Micronaut' comic book, which ran until 1986.

Not all of David Abrams' decisions proved to be so judicious: he rejected a deal to license toys for the upcoming motion picture *Star Wars*, famously arguing that Mego would go bankrupt if they produced toys based on every 'flash-in-the-pan' sci-fi B movie that came along. For a while 'Micronaut' figures sold so well that his decision seemed prudent. However, in time Kenner Products, who had picked up the baton, went on to make millions of dollars with their *Star Wars* action figures.

Perhaps Mego had learned a salient lesson, because after turning down *Star Wars* the company keenly acquired the rights to other new sci-fi movies and were soon manufacturing action figures associated with *Buck Rogers in the 25th Century*, *The Black Hole*, and *Star Trek: The Motion Picture*.

Playmates Toys' 'Lara Croft, Tomb Raider' and motorcycle date from 2001.

Pirates of the Caribbean
action figures: Zizzle (2004).

BELOW: **'Charlie Bucket'** from
*Charlie and the Chocolate
Factory*: Funrise (2005).

BELOW: **'Charlie Bucket'** from
*Charlie and the Chocolate
Factory*: Funrise (2005).

World War II-Themed Military Action Figures

In 1976, Mego had begun to produce a small collection of World War II-themed military action figures; these were marketed in France and Italy under the Polistil brand name, and in Germany, Australia and the United Kingdom under a variety of others, the most famous being Lion Rock, the name of Mego's manufacturing arm. These figures were released in the United States in the early 1980s as 'Johnny Action' or 'Combat Man'. All of them were half the size of the original 12-inch GI Joe format, which had lost its popularity.

A series of 3-inch tall diecast action figures, called 'Eagle Force', was Mego's final large product line, available between 1981 and 1982. Marketed as a counter-terrorist task unit, 'Eagle Force''s intended message was that the United States wasn't going to be pushed around any more, in keeping with the practice and policies of new president Ronald Reagan.

Hasbro *Marvel* Legends Movies *Iron Man Mark 1* 'Ironman': 6-inch action figure 'Iron Man' (2008).

Hasbro *Raiders of the Lost Ark* 'Indiana Jones' figure (2008).

But there was still life in the intermediate 8-inch format, and Mego signed an agreement with Palitoy's Bradgate division in the UK, and via their Lion Rock operation with Madelman and Polistil in Europe, to produce the 'Little Big Man' series and its derivatives such as 'Heroes of World War II', which achieved considerable success on the continent.

The End of the Road for Mego

When Mego was at its peak, it felt confident enough to branch out into new lines, such as the 2-XL toy robot and the 'Fabulous Fred' hand-held game player. Disappointingly, sales did not repay the company's investment, and with costs rising and revenues declining, inevitably Mego fell into debt. The 1982 financial year saw the company report losses of between $18 and $20 million, and that February the remaining staff were let go and the Mego offices closed. On 14 June 1982, Mego filed for Chapter 11 bankruptcy; the company officially went under in 1983.

But that wasn't the end of Mego or Martin ('Marty) Abrams and to keep hold of what he and his family had established, in 1986 he co-founded Abrams Gentile Entertainment (AGE) and endeavoured to reclaim the Mego trademark. It took him until early 2009 to do it, but he eventually succeeded.

In July 2018, the revived Mego Corporation announced that they were to produce a limited run of their classic style clothed action figures in their traditional 1/9 scale supplemented by some further 1/5 scale figures.

At the time of writing, the fact that Mego Corp, now called Marty Abrams Presents Mego, is intent on a significant return to the world of action figures is confirmed by the vigour of its legendary founder, now well into his seventh decade, but introducing new product to the market as actively as he had done fifty years ago.

MADELMAN

Established by friends Josep Maria Arnau and Andrés Campos, Spanish manufacturer Madelman (Plastic Industries Madel) began making 6-inch posable, articulated dolls in 1968, choosing that size so their products would fit easily into the pockets of children. One of the less well-known manufacturers of action figures, Madelman's designs would undoubtedly have had far greater impact on the world of action figures if they had been the product of a US company and not that of a small Spanish business. Nevertheless, amongst fans their figures, which first appeared in Spanish toy shops over the Christmas period in 1968, are held in high esteem – especially the rarer early ones: these featured 'crystal eyes' and simple pegged feet, on to which boots were easily push-fitted. Throughout the 1970s Madelman figures were further improved by the addition of hand-painted eyes and more sophisticated articulated feet.

Soon, a wide range of action figures and accessories was available. The supplementary parts are of note because they were of high quality, and although small in size, often utilized a composite of mixed materials for their manufacture, such as wood and metal for example, rather than relying on a paint finish to replicate full-size objects.

The variety of Madelman figures was diverse and included astronauts, pirates, cowboys, military figures, deep sea divers, superheroes, Eskimos and even a Kenyan-based safari scene that came complete with hunter, fez-wearing porter and a caged lion. Madelman horses and figures were also supported by an equally extensive vehicle range, including jeeps, helicopters and various wagons.

Madelman Spain exported its figures throughout Europe. The massive North American market was supplied by a subsidiary in Mexico, Exin Mex, and these items are particularly valued by collectors.

Sadly the original business ceased trading in 1983. For a while the Madelman baton was picked up by another Spanish business, Popular de Juguetes (PDJ), who, for a period, began to market versions of the original figures. These proved far less popular than authentic Madelman figures, and are consequently cheaper than the rarer vintage versions.

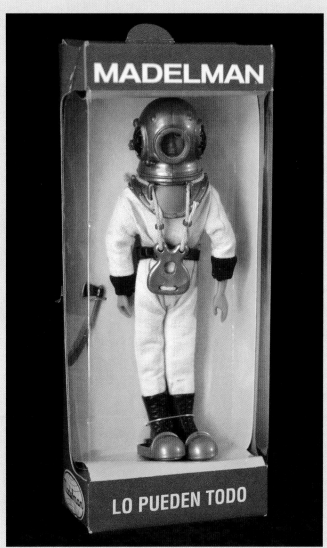

Madelman 'Diver' action figure from Spain. The box says, 'They can do it all.' (2004).

LION ROCK

Lion Rock was the manufacturing arm of Mego Corporation, and was also employed to distribute items in Europe, where Mego retained a sales agent to cover the Continent.

Lion Rock is especially remembered for its 'Micronaut' figures as well as a variety of World War II figures, especially 6-inch scale figures that came complete with authentically styled uniforms and accessories; these

were sold under various brand names such as 'Combat Man', 'Battle Brigade', 'War Heroes' and 'Johnny Action'.

Lion Rock made other types of figure, although these are less well known than their military offerings. Sports figures such as 'Steve Goal Getter', and especially their figure of Franz Beckenbauer, are now very highly sought after by collectors.

Lion Rock 'Sheriff' action figure (1975).

HIT ENTERTAINMENT

HIT Entertainment Ltd, or HiT as its branding is styled, is a British-American entertainment company owned by Mattel and originally established as 'hit!' in 1982. Henson International Television, to give it its full name, was developed from the production company of the late Jim Henson, of 'Muppets' puppetry fame, and now owns and distributes children's television series such as *Barney and Friends*, *Bob the Builder*, *Thomas and Friends*, *Fireman Sam* and *Angelina Ballerina*.

In early 2010, HiT licensed *Thomas and Friends* to Mattel for toys; in 2011, owners Apax Partners sold HiT Entertainment to Mattel Inc for $680 million. In March 2016, HiT was transferred to Mattel Creations, a division of Mattel formed to bring all content creation entities together.

PLAYMATES TOYS

Playmates Toys was founded as Playmates Industrial in Hong Kong in 1966 by Chan Tai Ho (later known as Sam Chan), and began life as a small manufacturing subcontractor for foreign toy producers. After almost a decade making generic dolls and pre-school toys for other toy companies, in 1975 Playmates took an important step towards becoming an independent toy producer and established a division to produce and market its own line of pre-school toys, opening an American subsidiary in Boston two years later.

To compete in the promotional toy market, a new California subsidiary named Playmates Toys Inc. was opened in 1983, and in 1984 Playmates Industrial went public, trading shares on the Hong Kong stock exchange under the new name Playmates Holdings Ltd.

In 1986 Playmates had their first big success in promotional toys with 'Cricket', a talking electronic baby doll. However, Playmates Toys entered the big league in the toy industry in 1988 when it purchased the licence to manufacture action figures based on the *Teenage Mutant Ninja Turtles* comics. These 'heroes in a half shell' were a massive success, propelling Playmates forwards, and in 1990 they became the first toymaker in history to net more than $100 million in one year.

Released in 1990, the first *Teenage Mutant Ninja Turtles* movie grossed more than $135 million, and that year the 'Turtles' had captured more than 60 per cent of the action-figure sector; it was estimated that 90 per cent of American boys under ten owned at least one 'Ninja Turtle'.

Sales of the 'Turtles' inevitably tailed off, but Playmates had something in the wings that they hoped might replace them. In 1991 they introduced 'Waterbabies', a range of water-filled dolls invented by American Dan Lauer, who as a child had fun filling rubber gloves with water and drawing faces on them. Despite initial reservations, Playmates purchased the licence, selling in excess of two million 'Waterbabies' in 1991 alone.

Playmates went from strength to strength, acquiring the licences for major movies such as *Star Trek: The Next Generation* and *Space Jam*.

In the late 1990s Playmates enjoyed huge success with a range of electronic toys: the 'Nano Pals' were electronic pets that responded to petting, feeding and being reprimanded – there were even talking 'Nano Pals' and 'Nano Fighters', a toy specifically aimed at boys. Playmates shared this lucrative market with Japan's Bandai, makers of the famous 'Tamagotchis'.

ABOVE: **Playmates 'Teenage Mutant Ninja' (1984) and 'Teenage Mutant Hero Turtle' (1987). Their name was changed to appease the British market where it was thought 'Ninja' might encourage schoolyard violence.**

RIGHT: **Playmate Toys, *Seaquest* 'DSV Commander Jonathan Devin Ford' (1993).**

CHARACTER GROUP PLC

Since its foundation in 1991, Britain's Character Group plc engaged in the design, development and international distribution of toys and games. In 2003, rather than relying on those sourced by third parties, the business took the decision to design some of its own products, and today over 75 per cent of all merchandise marketed by the group is developed in-house. This strategy has naturally resulted in significant export and import opportunities for the business, which now has offices in London, Manchester, Hong Kong and China, and employs nearly 250 people.

At the time of writing, Character's brands included Disney's 'Frozen', 'Doctor Who', 'Fireman Sam', 'Minecraft', 'My Little Pony', 'Peppa Pig', 'Postman Pat', 'Scooby Doo', 'Teksta', 'The Simpsons', and that old favourite and one-time Airfix

Character Group 'HM Armed Forces Royal Navy
Diver' (2009).

Character Group 'HM Armed Forces RAF Fast
Jet Pilot' (2009).

(and Playskool in the USA) staple, 'Weebles'.

Character Group is perhaps best known amongst action-figure enthusiasts for the 2009 release of its 'HM Armed Forces' toys. Writing about this range of authentic British fighting personnel, in May 2009 *The Daily Telegraph* said the toys were 'intended to fill the gap in the market left by figures popular with youngsters in the past such as "Action Man".' A spokesman for the Ministry of Defence added: 'We are rightly proud to be celebrating our Armed Forces through the production of these new action figures. These toys showcase our people and equipment, and this commercial recognition proves the high-level support for our forces among the British public.'

These action figures were manufactured in conjunction with the Army, the Royal Navy and the RAF to ensure that the camouflage gear and weapons

Character Group 'Dalek Ironside' (2010).

were authentic. The range included a 'Royal Marine Commando', an 'Army Infantryman' and an 'RAF Fast Jet Pilot'.

The 'Army Infantryman' action figure was equipped with an SA80A2 assault rifle, personal role radio, Kevlar flak-jacket body armour, and a Mark 4 Alpha Kevlar ballistic protection helmet with standard-issue goggles, and wore desert camouflage combats. The 'Royal Marine Commando' figure naturally sported the unit's acclaimed green beret. The 'Royal Air Force Fast Jet Pilot' figure appeared in full flight gear including white leather flying gloves, 'bone dome' flying helmet with oxygen mask, and survival-issue service pistol for use behind enemy lines.

IN A GALAXY, FAR, FAR AWAY: *STAR WARS'* FIGURES REIGN SUPREME

Kenner 1977 'Vintage Star Wars Tusken Raider (Sand People) 12-Back'. Because no one expected the movie to be such a phenomenal success, only limited *Star Wars* merchandise was available for several months after the film's debut. Kenner responded to the sudden demand for toys by selling boxed vouchers in its 'empty box' Christmas 1977 campaign. Initially, twelve *Star Wars* figures were released. The term '12-Back' refers to the first twelve figures shown on the back of the card.

Long before he graduated from the School of Cinematic Arts at the University of Southern California, science fiction had been an abiding interest of George Lucas. He was especially beguiled by the melodramatic classics of the 1930s, movie series such as *Flash Gordon* and *Buck Rogers*.

THX 1138, Lucas's first professional film, was pure sci-fi and a development of a project he had worked on at film school. However, it was the surprising success of his second venture in 1973, *American Graffiti*, which banked more that $100 million worldwide, that encouraged him to revive an idea he had long harboured for a trilogy of films entitled *The Star Wars*, a kind of Western set in outer space.

George Lucas and *Star Wars*

A traditional story of good versus evil transposed against an exciting inter-stellar background, Lucas was confident it would be a winner. Unfortunately his enthusiasm was not shared by the traditional Hollywood studios, who saw little merit in his project – its name now shortened to the more familiar 'Star Wars'. After being turned down by most of the major players in Hollywood, it is perhaps fitting that help came in the form of Alan Ladd Jr, son of the star of seminal Western *Shane*, the quintessential 1953

Western about salvation being the reward for those who follow a righteous path.

Star Wars Merchandizing: A Far-Sighted Deal

At the time Ladd was Head of Creative Affairs at 20th Century Fox, and in a position to green light projects he was confident would produce a return on his company's investment. It is the stuff of legend that George Lucas's agent, buoyed by the success his client had enjoyed following *American Graffiti*, approached Ladd, saying he felt Lucas deserved more than the traditional split of $200,000 ($100,000 for director and $50,000 each for Lucas's role as both writer and

'Even a ferocious RANCOR MONSTER needs someone to watch over him and be his friend. So here's your chance to get a RANCOR KEEPER free,' promised this 1984 advertisement. 'All you have to do is simply buy any six Action Figures and cut out the names from the front of the packs.'

producer). But although Ladd was sympathetic to the demand, there simply wasn't enough in the budget to pay any more.

However, Lucas was determined to maintain control of his progeny, and the right to make the two sequels he believed were essential to the story, and as negotiations continued, 20th Century Fox offered him a share of the merchandizing rights for *Star Wars*. Up until then, these rights had been of little interest to the studios. Lucas is on record as saying:

> When I took over the licence, I simply said I'm going to be able to make T-shirts, I'm going to be able to make posters, and I'm going to be able to sell this movie, even though the studio won't. So I managed to get control of pretty much everything that was left over that the studio didn't really care about.

At the time of writing, this iteration of a 1983 Kenner Han Solo '65-Back' has sold for as much as $600 in the USA.

A selection of mint boxed and carded Kenner 'Star Wars' action figures produced in association with 1983's *The Return of the Jedi*.

'Star Wars' *Return of the Jedi* advertisement: 'This is THE EMPEROR – symbol of the Dark Side of THE FORCE, master of DARTH VADER and the terrible IMPERIAL STORMTROOPERS, the very centre of the Empire's web of fear!'

And this, of course, included toy merchandizing. The agreement proved to be one of the most far-sighted deals in movie history.

Before *Star Wars*, merchandizing had been considered small beer in Hollywood, and regularly proved to be an albatross around the necks of those who signed such agreements, especially to franchisees who were obliged to invest in the design and manufacture of stock associated with a movie, and to pay an upfront premium to the studios. So back then, 20th Century Fox's insouciance was not surprising. But it was to prove a major mistake, because to date the toy merchandizing alone has brought in more than $20 billion for Lucas, far exceeding cinema receipts.

However, despite Lucas's unique agreement, success with *Star Wars* merchandizing wasn't guaranteed. The biggest fans of the movie were naturally youngsters, and although children were eager to bring the experi-

ence home with them, the success of the movie took everyone by surprise. With so many fantastic characters, both human and alien, and a plethora of robots and droids, action figures were a natural spin-off. However, prior to *Star Wars*' 1977 release, few toy manufacturers were interested. Indeed Mego, a US company enjoying success with action figures based on sci-fi properties such as *Star Trek* and *Buck Rogers in the 21st Century*, turned down flat the proposal made by Lucas Films' Head of Merchandizing, Charles Lippincott, when he approached them and offered them the action-figure licence.

In fact only one toy manufacturer, Kenner Products, took up the challenge, and that was largely down to the foresight of Bernard Loomis – but they acquired the licence so late in the day they weren't

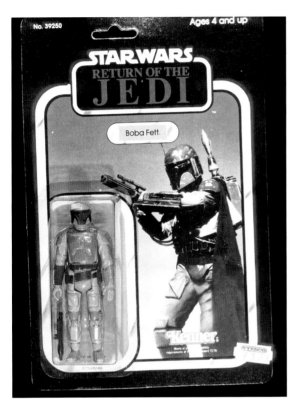

This *Return of the Jedi* 'Boba Fett' action figure cost £1.49 in Tesco in 1983. In December 2015, one sold for $938 in a Sotheby's auction.

Star Wars Collectors Series 12-inch 'Luke Sky Walker in Bespin Fatigues' (1996).

able to get toys to market by Christmas 1977 (the movie premiered in May that year).

Kenner Takes up the Manufacturing Challenge

Incredibly, Kenner resorted to a cunning plan, selling vouchers and promissory notes, which, upon receipt, guaranteed action figures by February or March of the following year. Just how youngsters felt when they tore off the wrapping paper from a package that contained nothing save an Early Bird Certificate assuring the eventual delivery of toy treasure is hard to imagine. Naturally, the twelve action figures from this initial batch are amongst the most prized items amongst action-figure collectors.

FAO Schwarz, the oldest toy shop in the USA, exclusive Star Wars Action Collection 12-inch 'Wedge Antilles' and 'Biggs Darklighter'.

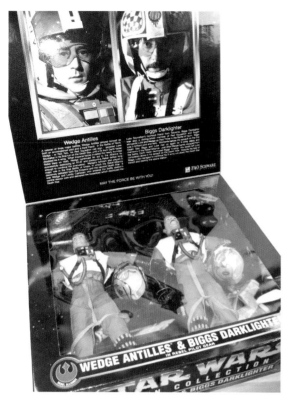

FAO Schwarz *Star Wars* Action Collection 'Wedge
Antilles' and 'Biggs Darklighter' in rebel pilot gear.

In 1985 Kenner ceased production of 3-inch figures
associated with the initial *Star Wars* trilogy, but
between 1978 and 1985 the company had produced
more than 300 million toys. Said Lucas famously:

> I'm just the movie guy, but the branding and the
> licensing and that sort of thing, it's fun. I like that
> there's lots of great toys and funny T-shirts and
> really great gadgets and things that are fun. … But
> at the same time, my main focus is on just making
> the movie.

Nevertheless despite his casualness there is no doubt
that Lucas knew exactly how to get the most out of his
movie franchise, and give something that fans could
take home and enjoy long after the credits faded.
Having signed away billions in additional revenues,
Fox are naturally kicking themselves for their over-
sight.

Another First: The 3-inch Figure Size

Interestingly, right from the start, *Star Wars* figures
were destined to be accompanied by replicas of the
innumerable space ships that abound in the movies,
and because of their scale relationship to the figures,
Lucas scored another first when he initiated the now
established trend for 3-inch figures as opposed to
the industry standard of 12-inch figures. Certainly
when he was first thinking of merchandise, George
Lucas assumed that his figures would follow the GI
Joe/Action Man model, but he soon realised that
'X-Wing', 'Speeders' and 'Tie Fighters', to say nothing
of the 'Star Destroyer', would have to be massive, and
consequently would be unaffordable if they were to
accompany 'standard'-size action figures; therefore
the smaller 3-inch figure size was settled upon.

Hasbro *Star Wars – Revenge of the Sith* – 'Force
Battlers Han Solo' (2005).

12-inch 'Qui-Gon Jinn' action figure from *Star Wars Episode I*: Hasbro (1999).

In 1999 *Star Wars Episode I – The Phantom Menace*, had its premier sixteen years after *The Return of the Jedi (Episode VI)*. Unmask the one queen – 'Queen Amidala' – and her hidden majesty, 'Anakin Skywalker' and 'Qui-Gon Jinn' large-scale figures (Hasbro).

ABOVE: Hasbro *Star Wars: Episode I* 3-inch figures. 'Amidala', 'Obi Wan Kenobi' and 'Darth Maul' each came complete with a 'Comm Talk Chip', which doubled up as a stand and, with the addition of a separately sold chip reader, enabled the figures to recount electronically phrases from the movie.

Selection of assorted *Star Wars: Episode I* 3-inch figures (Hasbro 1999).

Kenner Builds on *Star Wars* Success

The success of *Star Wars* in 1977 was unprecedented, and even took Lucas by surprise. After Kenner had purchased the licence for a flat fee of $100,000, as we have seen, they were unable to meet the huge demand by Christmas 1977. In 1978, Kenner brought out a further four action figures from the movie's

'Cantina' scene to accompany the initial dozen, and soon after that the line grew to twenty items. It was to increase exponentially over the next few years.

Initially, each figure was blister-packaged on to a 6 × 9-inch card, the reverse of which illustrated the other figures in the range and encouraged fans to collect them all. The first cards were known as '12-Backs' and featured, as the term suggests, the twelve figures then

Star Wars: Episode I Darth Maul vs. Obi-Wan Kenobi The Final Lightsaber Duel with 'Break Apart Darth Maul'. Hasbro (1999).

Star Wars: Episode I 'Jar Jar Binks' action figure with 'Gungan Battle Staff'. Hasbro (1999).

Hasbro 12-inch 'Sergeant Jyn Erso' ('Jedha') from *Rogue One* (2016).

GALOOB

Lewis Galoob Toys, Inc. was founded in 1957 by Lewis Galoob and his wife, Barbara Frankel. Headquartered in South San Francisco, California, today they are perhaps best known for creating 'Micro Machines', the tiny 1:160-scale vehicles and playsets; but they began life as a small distributor of toys and stationery. The company was incorporated in 1968.

Galoob's first real toy success was the reintroduction of a battery-powered 'Jolly Chimp', a cymbal-banging monkey toy first introduced by the Japanese company Daishin CK in the 1950s and sold under the brand name 'Musical Jolly Chimp'. When its head was pressed, Galoob's improved version nodded, screeched and bared its teeth.

In 1970 Lewis Galoob relinquished his position as president of the company, due to poor health, and his twenty-one-year-old son, David, took over the family business. In partnership with his brother Robert, Galoob's vice president, the pair aggressively pursued new product development, transforming the small company into a $1 million business by 1976.

Galoob continued to prosper, and in 1998, American

Galoob *A-Team* action figures (1983).

toy giant Hasbro purchased it for $220 million, retaining the Galoob name as one of Hasbro's brands. From 2005, the name 'Galoob' began appearing on Hasbro products, with the logo adorning the premium 'Titanium Series' diecast metal collectables, as well as a variety of other items including 'Transformers', 'Star Wars' and 'Battlestar Galactica'.

available. Quite soon the card backs showed twenty different figures, and before long this had multiplied to sixty-five, though by then each successive figure was denoted by an individual code rather than a

Hasbro 12-inch 'Rey (Jakku)' action figure from *The Force Awakens* (2015).

photograph. By the end of the year, Kenner had sold more than forty million of these figures, and achieved gross sales of more than $100 million.

Further Developments

Hasbro *Star Wars* Action Figures

In 2010, Hasbro began releasing modern *Star Wars* action figures with packaging reminiscent of the original Kenner 1978–1984 'Star Wars' product line. 'Star Wars: The Vintage Collection' is composed of new highly posable figures, with screen-accurate likenesses. Hasbro had done this twice before, with the 2004 'vintage' Original Trilogy Collection and the 2006–2007 'vintage' Saga Collection, but this is the first time that their 'Star Wars' line was entirely dedicated to replica Kenner carded figures.

LJN

LJN Toys was founded in 1970 by Jack Friedman, the name 'LJN' coming from the initials of Lewis J. Norman, the reverse of Norman J. Lewis, whose toy company Friedman had worked for as a sales representative in the 1960s. Lewis initially backed the company financially, but later sold his interest to a Chinese investor.

In an effort to retain more profits from the merchandizing of their film properties, in 1985 MCA/Universal acquired LJN for $66 million, the toy company having specialized in toys licensed to television and cinema properties.

LJN was already well known for its WWF wrestling figures, but the year of its acquisition it enjoyed a major success with action figures based on *ThunderCats*, the American animated television series that followed the adventures of a group of cat-like humanoid aliens.

In 1990, MCA sold LJN to Acclaim Entertainment. Acclaim phased out the toy lines, encouraging LJN to increase the number of electronic games it published for Nintendo on such platforms as the Super Nintendo Entertainment System and Game Boy. In 1995, LJN was folded into Acclaim proper, but was revived in 2000 to publish one Sega Dreamcast title, 'Spirit of Speed '37'.

LJN 'Gremlins' (1984) and 'ET' (1982) action figures.

Rare carded LJN 'Michael Jackson' stage outfit (1984).

The advent of the 'Star Wars' 3-inch figures in the mid-seventies was a huge success and finally put paid to the popularity of the traditional 12-inch figures of the Action Man type. However, although accessories such as vehicles and weapon systems were far cheaper than they had ever been with Action Man, the smaller figures themselves were too small to be embellished with much in the way of personal accessories, and certainly weren't suitable for a costume change or anything like that.

An 8-inch Scale for Action Figures

An interim scale for action figures was needed. Fortunately, manufacturers such as Mego came to the rescue with a range of 8-inch or thereabouts action figures. Other manufacturers such as Mattel chose 6 inches for their hugely successful 'Masters of the Universe' ('MOTU') range. Though more closely associated with plastic construction kits, in 1982 Revell released the short-lived 'Power Lords' range, which

Hasbro *Star Wars* 'Rey Jedi Training' action figure from *The Last Jedi* (2017).

Hasbro 12-inch Finn and Stormtrooper action figures from *The Force Awakens* (2015).

SIDESHOW COLLECTABLES

Sideshow Collectables began in 1994 and started out by creating action-figure prototypes for major toy companies such as Mattel and Galoob. In 1999, Sideshow began marketing its own line of figures under the Sideshow brand, beginning with the 'Universal Classic Monsters' 8-inch action-figure licence, which sold through Toys "R" Us and other mass-market retailers. The company then began to create items in the classic one-sixth scale format beloved of fans of Action Man and GI Joe; companies such as Dragon were discovering that these enjoyed a substantial market amongst fans who remembered the toys during their heyday, and newcomers looking for a tangible alternative to the virtual world of smartphones, tablets and laptops.

Sideshow has since forged collaborative relationships with a variety of Hollywood filmmakers and special-effect houses to produce some of the most sought-after collectables, including pre-production film maquettes from movies including *Iron Man*, *Transformers*, *The Avengers*, *Hellboy*, *Predators*, *Alien 3* and *Alien vs Predators*.

Sideshow Collectables currently partners with Marvel, Disney, WB, Lucasfilm, DC, Blizzard Entertainment and others to create product from properties such as *The Marvel Universe*, *The DC Universe*, *Star Wars*, *Alien & Predator*, *Terminator*, *The Lord of the Rings*, *G.I. Joe*, *Halo*, *World of Warcraft*, *Star Craft II*, *Mass Effect 3*, *Diablo 3*, and many more.

At the time of writing, licensed brands included 'James Bond', 'Friday the 13th', 'Indiana Jones and the Kingdom of the Crystal Skull', 'Jaws', 'Jurassic Park', 'Spider-Man 3', 'Star Wars', 'Teenage Mutant Ninja Turtles', 'The Terminator' and 'Tron: Evolution'.

Left to right: In *Return of the Jedi* a Gamorrean Guard was famously eaten by the Rancor monster inhabiting the pit beneath Jabba the Hutt's palace. 'Chief Chirpa', leader of the Ewoks on the forest moon of Endor in *Return of the Jedi*. Jabba the Hutt's pasty-faced major domo, the 'Twi'lek Bib Fortuna'. The emperor's Royal Guard Élite: red-helmeted and red-cloaked storm troopers who serve as Emperor Palpatine's personal bodyguards.

featured a very novel innovation allowing owners to get two figures for the price of one – a twist of each figure's body would result in a new appearance as the head and torso flipped through 180 degrees. Other figure ranges in this interim size included Tonka's 'Supernaturals', LJN's 'ThunderCats' and Kenner's 'The Real Ghostbusters'.

Manufacturers such as LJN and Mezco Toyz took the size of action figures to new heights, being responsible for figures of the 'Lion-O' character from *ThunderCats*, for example, to figures as large as 14 inches, and even a whopping 15 inches (38cm) tall.

So in a roundabout way, George Lucas is also responsible for the fact that collectors of action figures now enjoy the widest range of scales to choose from, everything from the 'Star Wars' 3-inch (or more properly 3¼-inch), through 5-inch, 6-inch, 10-inch and, of course, the original 12-inch format.

LJN 'ThunderCats' catalogue. Originally animated in Japan, the *ThunderCats* TV series ran from 1985 to 1989.

'ThunderCats Evil Mutants' page from the LJN catalogue.

CONDITION, VALUES AND WHERE TO BUY

Assessing Condition

For any collectable, condition is fundamental to financial value. Philatelists expect stamp designs to be centred within the perforated borders and to feature perforations that are in pristine condition. Similarly, collectors of rare books look for examples complete with dust wraps and with pages free from foxing. Postcard collectors dismiss items featuring creases or worn corners. And so on, and so on.

Collectors of action figures are no exception to this rule and expect the best, shunning damaged packaging, scruffy outfits, missing accessories and blemished facial features. Regardless of its vintage, if an action figure is in a poor state, its worth will be greatly reduced.

It is hardly surprising, therefore, that the vintage collectables worth the most are so-called mint-in-box (MIB) and mint-on-card (MOC) examples. One toy dealer I used to buy from, rather disparagingly called such pristine items 'failed toys', because they had obviously never been played with and subjected to the rough-housing children are expected to inflict on such amusements.

Immaculate examples of toys from more than thirty-odd years ago are now very few and far between. 'Back in the day' it was the custom for the, usually young, recipient of a new toy such as a diecast toy or action figure, to quickly dispose of the packaging, keeping only the contents. It's only in recent times that buyers have treated their purchases with kid gloves, preserving the packaging and retaining it in good order.

Obviously, some tidier children did maintain their toys flawlessly, protecting their GI Joe or Action Man by putting them neatly back in their original packaging after they had played with them. Otherwise, how would such perfect examples from long ago have survived? Perhaps they endured because they had been consigned to storage in the loft or garage – maybe they had been unwelcome gifts in the first place. Remarkably, therefore, some boxed figures from as long as half a century ago survive in good condition and are still with us today.

Matchbox Stingray and Troy Tempest action figure (1993).

Carded accessories are another matter, however. Whereas figures can be repeatedly removed from their boxes and placed back in them without damaging the flap and panel closures of the carton, removing accessories from their backing cards is less easy and almost inevitably results in the destruction of said packaging. Figures from the 1960s or before – like, for example, those of A. C. Gilbert – feature accessories displayed on carded packaging usually secured by thread on to a backing card sealed in cellophane or in polythene bags. These can be relatively easily replaced and repaired – so collectors of allegedly original items should beware. Those from the 1970s up to the present, however, are generally contained in transparent, vacuum-formed polystyrene 'blister'

Based on Hugh Lofting's series of books published in the 1920s, Doctor Dolittle first appeared in letters written to his children when the author was serving in the trenches during the First World War. In 1967, Rex Harrison starred in Richard Fleischer's hit movie. The same year Mattel released a 6-inch bendy figure of the famous doctor and his parrot Polynesia.

packaging, from which items can rarely be removed without destroying the packaging.

With the value of classic 'Star Wars' figures now achieving stratospheric levels, unscrupulous dealers often resort to repurposing loose figures, cleaning them up and sandwiching them between a once-removed transparent blister and a repro backing card. If the job is done neatly enough, it can be all but impossible to detect such fakery.

Today, many enthusiasts avail themselves of two of everything they buy, consigning one example to immediate storage. But this sort of behaviour is somewhat misguided. With so many items being carefully conserved, the number of things saved for posterity increases exponentially, and items survive in contradiction to the natural order of things. With so many survivors in circulation, their rarity and consequent value has, ironically, reduced significantly.

The same goes for the current vogue for certificated limited editions. Often having paid a premium price, purchasers of these are almost obliged to carefully look after everything they've bought. Realistically, however, if all these remain intact, even an edition of *only* 10,000 worldwide will individually probably be worth less in the long term than they cost originally.

Cleaning and Rejuvenating Action Figures

However, regardless of how they are curated, over time action figures, either loose or complete with their original packaging, can deteriorate, becoming grubby or discoloured. Adhesive residue from price labels and remnants of sticky tape can disfigure boxes. Clothes can become stained, accessories damaged, and vinyl flesh sullied by the patina of years of grease from fingers or just plain and simple household dust.

Fortunately, two fluids are on hand to remedy most of these afflictions: good old H_2O, and a light petroleum distillate, such as Ronsonal lighter fluid. The gentle application of a sheet of kitchen towel dipped in warm water, to which a small amount of detergent has been added, will ensure that grimy vinyl faces and hands come up very well. More stubborn marks can be removed with some gentle scrubbing with a soft toothbrush dipped in the warm soapy solution.

Grease and adhesive residue, on the other hand, can be easily removed by the application of lighter fluid, as can the residue of adhesive tape and price labels, the material's spirit base removing any unwanted marks and disfigurement in no time. I've

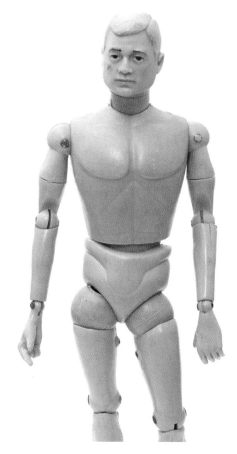

The earliest *Action Man* figures can be identified by their painted heads – flock hair was a long way off – and flesh-coloured painted metal rivets securing the joints of their limbs. The numerous articulations of the earliest *GI Joe* and *Action Man* figures were far in advance of anything their rivals could manage. However, over time such junctions were prone to loosening, and if the internal suspension holding everything together failed, they would completely collapse.

used lighter fluid since I was an art student, back in the late 1970s.

Back in those pre-pc days, in *every* sense, the Apple Macintosh wasn't available until 1984, professional and novice graphic designers like me were encouraged to wipe down their art board with kitchen towel soaked in lighter fluid, and thereby degrease the surface so that when a black line was drawn on it with a Rotring ink pen it was straight and true. Today, nearly forty years after I graduated, I still wouldn't be without one of the distinctive yellow cans.

Lighter fluid is not only invaluable for cleaning marks that prove impervious to water from action figures, but by gently saturating old price stickers or other unwanted embellishments from vintage packaging, such unwanted additions can simply be floated off. Any residue petroleum distillate will quickly evaporate, leaving the treated surface unblemished.

Dingy fabric uniforms and other costumes can also be rejuvenated by some careful remedial work. Whilst the vigorous action of a domestic washing machine might prove too robust for such delicate items, thank goodness for travel wash, those small bottles of concentrated liquid detergent that provide a gentler treatment than washing powder, and which start working immediately. Enthusiasts will be amazed at how much grime even the briefest soaking will remove. However, it is important to be careful not to damage any insignia that might be affixed by adhesive to uniforms. As far as drying is concerned, my advice is to lay out damp items on several sheets of clean kitchen towel, turning them over occasionally.

Certain items such as trousers and jackets might benefit from the gentle application of an eclectic iron, on its lowest heat setting. Again, be careful of any insignia that might be applied, because even the lowest heat will be enough to dissolve any adhesive securing badges, or stripes of medal ribbons.

Cleaning the vinyl surface of figures, renovating vintage packaging, and refreshing the fabric of the outfits of action figures are just some of the remedial steps necessary to restoring action figures to good condition. Sometimes the figures themselves are in a serious state of disrepair and require dramatic surgery to rejuvenate them.

As plastic ages, it sometimes begins to deteriorate. Although not as fugitive as some of the plastic compositions used on Marx action figures, especially the caramel-coloured material in the 'Best of the West' range, *Action Man* figures can suffer from stress fractures, as this photo shows. Collectors should ask to see unclothed photos of the anatomy of early figures to avoid purchasing a dud.

Repairing and Refurbishing Action Figures

Other than the distinctive caramel-coloured plastic used in the manufacture of some of Marx's 'Best of the West' figure ranges – which has an alarming propensity to crumble and snap, usually knee and elbow joints in particular – most other action figures can be disassembled and repaired without too much difficulty. Generally manufactured from acrylonitrile butadiene styrene (ABS), most action figures will survive being carefully prised apart by a knife from the cutlery drawer. Sometimes, before torso halves can be separated, rivets will need to be detached and small screws removed before the ingenious web of springs or elastic can be examined and any deficient components replaced.

Two other things are worth mentioning briefly here. Firstly, over time it has been found that combin-

ing two types of vinyl and the clear polythene used to enable the contents in window boxes to be readily viewed, can result in discoloration and degradation of one of the materials used. The grey 'zombie' heads on some Mego figures is a manifestation of this. Caution is also advised when trying to replace heads and limbs to early figures. The head of Gilbert's Moon McDare, for example, is secured to the torso with the addition of a hard-plastic rebated plug in his neck. More than half a century since it was manufactured, this element can turn brittle and shatter if care isn't taken.

The original 1964 Action Men had moulded vinyl-painted heads (which, over time, sometimes shrink and became unmalleable) and their limbs were fixed to their bodies by elastic with crimped metal eyelets through which rivets passed, metal hooks retaining the neck post and shoulders. Pre-1970 bodies used painted rivets similar to the earliest GI Joes, but later ones had chromed rivets that were not used on the Hasbro US version.

It is beyond the scope of this book to consider such refurbishment processes in detail. Anyway, numerous websites abound across the web, explaining such procedures as re-stringing Action Man arms using elastic and reattaching the springs to secure the limbs of vintage Marx figures, so anyone in search of authoritative advice is urged to search the treasure trove that is cyberspace.

Protecting and Displaying Action Figures

Whether in pristine condition straight from the box, or carefully conserved following some discreet repair work and the application of one or two repro parts, most action figures will be put on display – their owner's pride and joy. To exhibit them to their best and maintain them in good order, free of dust or the risk of accidental damage, several simple expedients are recommended. The first step is to protect figures by keeping them in an enclosed display cabinet or, perhaps, one of the many Perspex figurine cases featuring a one-piece lift-off top that fits snuggly over a generally thick black base. The best examples of these feature a discreet vent hole to prevent moisture or mould.

A wide range of sizes are commercially available. Collectors of vintage GI Joe and Action Man figures can avail themselves of cabinets that stand 14 inches tall and come complete with a waist-hold stand, designed to keep figures upright.

The larger action figures are notorious for their inability to stand on their own two feet, and to rectify this a range of proprietary display stands is available. Most of the designs on the market feature unobtrusive wire armatures that rise from a circular display base, and support the displayed figure around the waist. Alternatively, simple transparent bases can be employed that feature concealed raised mouldings designed to surround and support only one foot – all that is needed to keep a figure upright. Similar bases, featuring pegs that slot into circular apertures in the soles of smaller figures, can be equally useful.

Sourcing Vintage Action Figures

In the old days, collectors wanting to purchase vintage toys were obliged to select them from the faint pages of a catalogue duplicated on a Roneo machine, then, once a selection had been made, make a phone call to confirm the item was still in stock, post a cheque with the order to the dealer, and then wait patiently for up to a month before the longed-for item arrived. Compared to those days, today's enthusiasts have never had it so good.

The internet has changed everything, and because of it, eBay has reigned supreme – though as a BBC television presenter might say, other online auction sites are available. A cursory glance at eBay and its competitor sites reveals the most staggering values for vintage action figures, with mint examples, complete with their original packaging, achieving the highest prices.

The most expensive items aren't simply vintage GI Joe or Action Man figures and accessory sets. Complete Gilbert 'Moon McDare' action figures can easily outstrip Action Man 12-inch figures in price. Boxed versions of this classic, and other Gilbert figures such as Honey West and the duo from *Man from U.N.C.L.E.* achieve equally high prices, as do figures such as Marx's 'Stony Smith' and any of the 'Best of the West' range. Even relatively recent figures in the 'Masters of the Universe' ('MOTU') and 'ThunderCats' ranges can command top prices. And of course, some of the numerous 3-inch 'Star Wars' figures now achieve astronomic values.

Other great places to source vintage action figures include car boot sales and charity shops. But again, be warned: professional dealers are in the habit of scouring both such locations very early in the day, purchasing early bird tickets for the former and keeping a constant eye on new stock in charity shops.

In our modern world, with its plethora of television programmes about hidden treasures and the financial value of such vintage items, everyone thinks that anything old must be of high value, so it's quite hard to come across a figure that someone else hasn't seen first. But on occasions, bargains can still be found. The pursuit of treasure can be as much fun as its acquisition.

A Word of Caution

One final bit of advice concerning old and rare action figures that you think might be improved by remedial work or the addition of repro components. In the words of that well-known phrase, it is often best to leave well alone. Most collectors appreciate that anything of a significant vintage will exhibit the patina of age, and enthusiasts should be encouraged to refrain from changing, disturbing or unintentionally worsening any existing problems. So if in doubt, do nothing save to preserve the object in its current state, maintaining it for posterity and the enjoyment of future generations.

CHAPTER TEN

EPILOGUE: AND WHAT OF THE FUTURE?

Times change, and in this networked, multi-channel world, many of the pastimes and hobbies that previously fulfilled so many enthusiasts for so long have been forced to adapt if they are to survive. But despite competition from online video games, streamed media and myriad social media platforms, tradition continues – albeit that now modellers, for example, no longer have model shops from which to purchase, and traditional toy shops are increasingly dwindling in number.

Thank goodness for the internet, even if it is one of the main reasons that traditional retail channels have disappeared! The advent of online shopping has enabled access to a truly global market. Even if there is no longer a traditional bricks-and-mortar toy shop on your high street, there are now hundreds of thousands of virtual shops on infinite high streets across the globe. The opportunities for collectors are endless.

Fortunately, the market for action figures appears as strong as ever, and regardless of which platform new films, television series or video games are delivered on, fans still want tangible collectables to keep as mementos. Relatively inexpensive, durable, and easy to store and display, action figures endure as ideal souvenirs, many of them becoming true financial investments, worth many times more than their original purchase price after only a very few years.

Doubtless by the time this book appears a new gaming trend or Netflix blockbuster will have arrived on the scene, supported perhaps by a range of action figures of various sizes. But at the time of writing, the following three contemporary series have already generated a substantial following amongst fans, many of them having enhanced their devotion with the addition of associated action figures.

The first in my trio of recent successes is *Breaking Bad*, a television series that ran for five seasons, from January 2008 to September 2013. It tells the story of

Funko 'Reaction Breaking Bad Walter White' action figure (2015).

MEZCO TOYZ

Manufacturing a wide range of licensed action figures, Mezco Toyz was created by Michael Markowitz (Mez). One of the company's most popular product lines were the cult 10-inch tall dolls, packed in coffin-shaped boxes, made under licence to the *Living Dead* franchise, which were produced from the year 2000. Currently, Mezco's pop culture line is proving enormously popular: the One:12 Collective of 1:12 scale fully posable action figures manufactured in association with a huge variety of properties such as *Family Guy* and *South Park*, and with characters such as Hellboy and dozens of others right across both the Marvel and DC Universes, is proving enormously popular. Outside action figures and doll releases, Mezco is also known for its original block-style figures line: Mez-Itz and Mini Mez-Itz, the 2-inch collectable figures that now include Batman and Green Lantern, and neat two-packs that include pairings such as Batman/'The Joker, Hal Jordan'/'Sinestro' and Superman/'Mongul'. Mini Mez-Itz figures feature five points of articulation and are packaged together on a blister card.

Funko action figure of 'Brienne of Tarth', a knight of the House of Tarth and the only daughter of Lord Selwyn Tarth. A 'Game of Thrones Legacy' action figure (2019).

THREEZERO

Established in Hong Kong by Kim Fung Wong in 2000, Threezero action figures have achieved an enviable reputation for design and manufacturing quality. Featuring a striking gasmask logo designed by Michael Lau, who, along with Jason Siu and Elphonso Lam, also designs the brand's figures, Threezero started out making special forces figures which, uniquely, came equipped with diecast metal weapons.

Along with action figures licensed to properties including *The Walking Dead*, *The X Files*, *Bioshock 2*, *Game of Thrones* and *Ghost In The Shell*, Threezero has also teamed up with Japanese manufacturer Bandai to collaborate on a new mecha toy and 1/12th scale pilot designed by Kunio Okawara, who extended the ideas of legendary Japanese mecha anime creator, Yoshiyuki Tomino, for the hugely successful anthropomorphic Gundam robots.

Walter White (Bryan Cranston), a conflicted chemistry teacher who is diagnosed with lung cancer, and who, together with his former student Jesse Pinkman (Aaron Paul), becomes a drug dealer and starts making and selling crystallized methamphetamine to secure his family's financial future before he dies.

By the time the last episode of season five was broadcast, *Breaking Bad* had achieved the highest audiences of any cable show on American television, and received a host of awards, including numerous accolades for members of the cast. In 2013, *Breaking Bad* even secured an entry in the Guinness World Records to be celebrated as the most critically acclaimed show of all time. The principal licensees of action figures associated with the property were Mezco Toyz and Threezero.

FUNKO

Founded in 1998 by Mike Becker, and now led by CEO Brian Mariotti, Washington-based company Funko is now acknowledged as one of the leading purveyors of licensed popular culture vinyl figurines and bobbleheads. However, the US company also produces licensed plush action figures, and electronic items such as USB drives, lamps and headphones.

Funko was originally conceived as a small project to create various low-tech, nostalgia-themed toys – indeed, the first bobblehead the company manufactured was of the well-known restaurant icon, the 'Big Boy', mascot of the famous Big Boy Hamburger chain.

Since 2005, when Brian Mariotti took over, Funko has greatly extended the scope of its toy lines and increased the number of lucrative licensing deals with major companies. By 2012 the company had sold more than $20 million worth of merchandise.

To raise funds, in 2013 Funko was sold to Fundamental Capital, a private equity firm, and in late 2015 ACON Investments announced that it had purchased it from them. This corresponded with the company outgrowing its initial premises and moving into a 17,000-square-feet flagship store in downtown Everett in August 2017. The same year, Funko acquired British toymaker Underground Toys, which was also its European distributor.

Funko has created 13,642 different products in dozens of different toy lines since its inception. The first, 'Wacky Wobblers', is a line of bobbleheads depicting various characters, mainly from popular culture, such as 'Betty Boop', 'Cap'n Crunch' and 'The Cat in the Hat'. The company's mascot, a recurring character in the Funko franchise, is 'Freddy Funko'.

To encourage the collectability of its products, Funko periodically retires individual figures, doing what it calls 'vaulting'. A subsequent re-release of a 'vaulted edition' will be presented in distinctive packaging, thereby maintaining the integrity and relative value of the earlier item.

After a preview line of DC Comics characters was released at San Diego Comic-Con 2010, the Funko 'Pop!' line of products was fully revealed in 2011 at the New York Toy Fair. Funko's 'Pop!' vinyl line depicts licensed characters from franchises such as *Doctor Who*, *Marvel*, *DC*, *Disney*, *Star Wars*, *Wizarding World*, and other pop culture entities.

At the 2019 New York Toy Fair, billed as 'The largest toy, game and youth entertainment product marketplace in the Western Hemisphere', Funko announced a new line of 'Pop!' vinyls, 'Pop! Town', which would see classics from such franchises as *Ghostbusters* and *Scooby-Doo* packaged with familiar buildings associated with the character's storyline.

HBO's *Game of Thrones* is an adaptation of George R. R. Martin's *A Song of Ice and Fire* series of six fantasy novels, the first of which is *A Game of Thrones*. Each of the eight seasons of the blockbuster television show, which was produced and mainly filmed in Belfast, corresponded to one of Martin's novels (some of the novels were split into two parts). The success of the show was an enormous boost to Northern Ireland – it was produced in Belfast and mostly filmed in the province.

With its main theme the story of the civil wars between rival houses, each vying for the supreme 'Iron Throne', *Game of Thrones* also considered the grievances and disputes of individual characters such as Daenerys Targaryen, the daughter of King Aerys II Targaryen, Brienne, the daughter and only surviving child of Lord Selwyn Tarth, and Jon Snow, the illegitimate son of a Northern lord, the identity of whose mother viewers are kept guessing throughout the drama.

In the USA, the series premiered in April 2011, and concluded, to mixed reviews amongst die-hard fans, in May 2019; altogether there were seventy-three episodes spread across the eight seasons. Not surprisingly, with a character list rivalling Tolkien's *Lord of the Rings*, *Game of Thrones* offered manufacturers of action figures the widest imaginable scope, and the variety of items produced under licence to the

McFarlane Toys 7-inch 'Fortnite Drift' action figure. Drift is the first unlockable skin in the paid Battle Pass for Season 5 of *Fortnite* (2019).

RIGHT: McFarlane Toys 7-inch 'Fortnite Drift' action figure out in the open. The finish on this and other McFarlane action figures is remarkable.

In 1999, Florida-based Play Along Toys secured the licence for a Britney Spears doll line. The success of her first two studio albums, *Baby One More Time* (1999) and *Oops!... I Did It Again* (2000) made her the best-selling teenage artist of all time.

TOY BIZ (NOW MARVEL TOYS)

Toy Biz can be traced back to the late nineteenth century, and Chantex, a Canadian manufacturer of children's games and toys. A 1980 merger with Randim Marketing, a manufacturer and wholesaler of school supplies, resulted in a new name: Charan Industries Inc. In 1984 the businesses went public, and its Charan Toy Inc. subsidiary became one of the leading North American rights owners, holding licences for top brands, including the phenomenally successful 'Cabbage Patch Kids'.

In 1988 the business was reincarnated as Toy Biz, an American company. The new firm concentrated on creating toys based on Marvel Comics' cast of characters, including the 'Amazing Spider-Man', 'The Incredible Hulk', 'Captain America', 'Daredevil' and 'The Punisher'. In early 1991 Toy Biz released the first 'X-Men' line: 'Cyclops', 'Nightcrawler', 'Storm', 'Colossus', 'Wolverine' (brown costume) and 'Archangel'. Together with 'Juggernaut' and 'Apocalypse', the X-Men's nemesis, 'Magneto', comprised the baddies. Further 'X-Men' figures helped to confirm Toy Biz's status as a major player in the action-figures world. Eventually, Toy Biz launched 'Spider-Man Classic' and 'Marvel Legends', two enormously successful lines that helped to reinforce Marvel's toy presence.

With almost thirty points of articulation, these figures proved to be some of the most realistically posable figures ever made.

In 1993, in return for 46 per cent of its equity, Toy Biz secured an 'exclusive, perpetual, royalty-free licence' with Marvel. Access to a rich source of available characters and such an advantageous licensing deal meant that by 1995 Toy Biz's profit margins exceeded those of well-established toy firm Mattel.

By the mid-1990s, Marvel-related action figures and playsets generated about 50 per cent of Toy Biz's annual sales.

Toy Biz went on to manufacture the successful 'Revlon Fashion Dolls', once the province of Ideal Toys, and then to license some non-Marvel brands including 'Hercules: The Legendary Journeys' and 'Xena: Warrior Princess'. It established its 'Classic Heroes' candy division in early 1996, selling candy/toy combinations mainly based on Marvel characters. Following a licensing agreement with Apple Computers, in 1996 the company also entered the toy industry's electronic learning aids (ELA) sector.

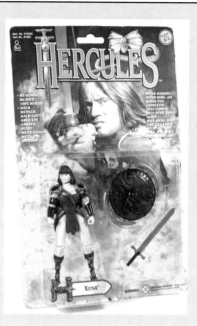

MOC Toy Biz 'Xena' from *Hercules* (1995).

Toy Biz's acquisition of the *The Lord of the Rings* toy line is possibly one of its greatest successes, closely followed by the licence for the World Championship Wrestling (WCW) figures, notable for their 'Smash'n'Slam' and 'Grip'n'Flip' wrestling figures as well as the 'Total Nonstop Action Wrestling' (TNA) series that followed.

By the late 1990s, financial complications at Marvel, a company founded in 1939 and which since the early 1960s had been the home of the legendary Stan Lee, forced it to restructure, and in June 1998 Marvel Enterprises was established, Toy Biz becoming an operating division within the new entity.

In January 2007, Hasbro acquired the exclusive right to be the official toy manufacturer of registered Marvel Entertainment characters, meaning that Marvel Toys would no longer be able to produce any Marvel figures as it would violate the Marvel Entertainment/Hasbro deal!

On 31 August 2009, The Walt Disney Company announced a deal to acquire Marvel Comics' parent corporation, Marvel Entertainment, for $4 billion, Marvel Enterprises becoming a wholly owned subsidiary of Disney Company. Marvel's former film subsidiary, Marvel Studios, is now also a subsidiary of Walt Disney Studios, where it currently develops and produces its own films based on *Marvel* characters. Toy Biz is now known by the appellation, Marvel Toys.

property has been remarkable. McFarlane Toys, Funko, Threezero and Dark Horse appear to have cornered the market for *Game of Thrones* action figures.

Developed by Epic Games and released in 2017, *Fortnite* is now one of the most successful online video games, attracting more than 200 million players worldwide. It is available in three distinct versions that otherwise share the same general gameplay and game engine: 'Fortnite: Save the World', a cooperative shooter-survival game for up to four players who are each encouraged to steadily build up their weaponry for use against zombie-like targets; 'Fortnite Battle Royale', a game where up to 100 players fight to the last; and 'Fortnite Creative', where players are given complete freedom to create bespoke worlds and battle arenas.

Fortnite Battle Royale became a resounding success, attracting a staggering 125 million-plus players before it was even a year old, and grossing hundreds of millions of dollars per month. McFarlane Toys and Epic Games won the prize for the manufacture of action figures associated with *Fortnite.*

The above is just my opinion of what might be a hot future collectable. There are others of course, including, for example, Marvel Legends' 12-inch Deadpool action figures by Hasbro based on the 2016 Marvel Comics superhero film. There are also Mattel's WWE (World Wrestling Entertainment, Inc.) Élite figures of wrestlers. I have even included a Boyzone figure and one of Britney Spears – the choice is yours. But if the current values for action figures that were manufactured as recently as only a decade ago are anything to go by, contemporary action figures are as worthy of laying down as fine Bordeaux, Burgundy or Rhône wines.

Vivid Imaginations' 12-inch action figure of Irish singer-songwriter and professional drift driver Shane Lynch, former member of boyband Boyzone (1995).

McFARLANE TOYS

After working with Mattel on action figures based on his comic book creations, in 1994 Canadian illustrator Todd McFarlane left the creators of Barbie to establish his eponymous toy business. Since then, McFarlane's sometimes uncompromising action figures have courted approbation and criticism in equal measure. That same year, the introduction of a line of characters based on his comic book *Spawn* raised the bar significantly as far as the design and production of action figures was concerned. We can thank McFarlane's efforts for the ultra-detailed toys we take for granted today.

Since the introduction of McFarlane Toys' *Spawn* figures, the business has expanded considerably and now features licensed products from other originators, so that today the company's inventory includes figures from *The Simpsons*, and the 'Movie Maniacs' horror range, which features the likes of 'Freddy Krueger', 'Michael Myers', 'The Terminator', 'Leatherface' and 'The Thing'. Other figures have been inspired by sporting legends or video games such as 'Metal Gear Solid'.

McFarlane has given traditional works a chilling twist with fairy tales and classics such as the *Wonderful Wizard of Oz* being given a unique makeover. To ensure authenticity, McFarlane has collaborated with individuals such as Clive Barker (*Hellraiser* and *Candyman*) and H. R. Giger (*Alien*).

Released biannually, 'McFarlane's Dragons' first appeared in 2005. Divided into different clans, sets featured several highly detailed 6-inch dragon action figures, and a slightly larger and more complex boxed-set figure. The series now includes numerous exquisite creators of such variety, their abundance has proved addictive for collectors.

A lifelong fan of the horror genre, in 1997 the company's founder introduced 'Todd McFarlane's Monsters Playsets'.

Countless other figures have appeared since, including 'Attila the Hun', gunslinger 'Billy the Kid', 'Rasputin', 'Jack the Ripper', 'Vlad the Impaler' ('Dracula'), 'Edward Scissorhands', and no less scary perhaps, figures based on rock legends KISS. In fact, in recent years McFarlane Toys has cornered the market in music industry-based action figures, producing miniatures of The Beatles, Alice Cooper, Ozzy Osbourne, Metallica, Slash, Iron Maiden's mascot Eddie, Jimi Hendrix, Freddie Mercury and Elvis Presley.

'McFarlane's Military' first appeared in 2005, when support for US soldiers serving overseas was at a peak and figures such as 'Army Ranger' or 'Navy Seal', each in full military gear, with highly detailed weapons and accessories, proved very popular with consumers.

More recently, franchises such as *Lost* and *The Walking Dead* have inspired McFarlane Toys to produce even newer and more elaborate figures.

McFarlane Halo Reach Comicon 'Exclusive Noble 7' action figure (2010).

ACTION FIGURES TOP THE BEST-SELLER CHARTS and BIBLIOGRAPHY

Action figures are now an inherent part of the world of toys, a fundamental component, and since their inception in the 1960s they have consistently topped the charts in terms of their popularity. There are numerous surveys revealing the most popular toys at any given time, but I have selected just three of them.

The first is the British Toy and Hobby Association's annual poll. Since 1965 the BTHA's Toy of the Year has been one of the determining factors behind which toys end up in gift wrap under the Christmas tree. This poll also frequently results in runs on toy shops, with the consequence that, to the frustration of parents, they often sell out of 'must-haves' long before the big day.

Another trusted measure, again from the UK, comes from retailer Argos – specifically, from their eponymous catalogue. Since it first appeared in 1973, this publication has provided a fascinating barometer of the most popular toys in Britain.

Finally, I have selected the survey from America's National Hall of Fame, an organization that has measured the relative success of different toys in the USA since 1965. This august body's records reveal that since they first appeared in the mid-1960s, action figures have consistently charted well.

British Toy and Hobby Association Toy of the Year

1966: Action Man (Palitoy)
1968: 'Sindy' (Pedigree Toys)
1970: 'Sindy' (Pedigree Toys)
1982: 'Star Wars' toys (Kenner)
1983: 'Star Wars' toys (Kenner)
1984: 'Masters of the Universe' (Mattel)
1985: 'Transformers' (Optimus Prime Hasbro/ Takara)
1986: 'Transformers' (Optimus Prime Hasbro/ Takara)
1990: 'Teenage Mutant Ninja Turtles' (Playmates Toys)
1992: 'WWF Wrestlers' (Hasbro)
1994: 'Power Rangers' (Bandai)
1996: Barbie (Mattel)
2008: 'Ben 10' action figures 10-inch and 15-inch (Bandai)

Argos Catalogue Top Toys Since 1973

1979: 'Star Wars' figures (Kenner)
1985: 'Transformers' (Hasbro/Takara)

1990: 'Teenage Mutant Hero Turtles' (Playmates Toys)

1992: Barbie (Mattel)

1994: 'Power Ranger Action Figures' (Bandai)

1996: 'Buzz Lightyear' action figure (Thinkway Toys)

2002: 'Bratz' dolls (MGA Entertainment)

America's National Toy Hall of Fame Most Popular Toys since 1965

1965: GI Joe (Hasbro)

1971: 'Weebles' (Playskool Toys)

1976: 'Sonny Bono' and 'Cher' dolls (Mego)

1977: 'Star Wars' action figures (Kenner)

1981: 'He-Man' from *Masters of the Universe* (Mattel)

1984: 'Transformers' (Hasbro/Takara)

1990: 'Teenage Mutant Ninja Turtles' (Playmates Toys)

1994: 'Mighty Morphin Power Rangers' (Bandai)

2001: 'Bratz' dolls (MGA Entertainment)

2016: 'Star Wars' BB-8 Droid (Sphero)

Bibliography

Baird, Frances *Action Man – The Gold Medal Book for Boys 1966–1984* (New Cavendish, 1996)

Bonavita, Tim *Mego Action Figure Toys* (Schiffer, 2001)

Ellis, Phil *Sci-fi & Fantasy Collectables* (Millers, 2003)

Gutzman, Kurt Vonn *Collect Them All! Confessions of a Recovering Action Figure Thief* (Gutzman, 2012)

Harrison, Ian *Action Man – The Official Dossier* (Collins, 2003)

Heaton, Tom *The Encyclopedia of Marx Action Figures* (Krause Publications, 1999)

King, Kevin *Action Man – The Real Story 1966–1996* (Cairo Café Publications Limited, 2000)

Manos, Paris and Susan *Collectable Action Figures* (Collector Books, 1996)

Manos, Paris and Susan *Collectable Male Action Figures*, Collector Books, 1996

Marshall, John *Action Figures of the 1960s* (Schiffer, 1998)

Michlig, John *GI Joe: The Complete Story of America's Favourite Man of Action* (Chronicle Books, 1998)

Rich, Mark *Toys A to Z* (Krause Publications, 2001)

Santelmo, Vincent *The Complete Encyclopedia to GI Joe – 3rd Edition* (Krause Publications, 2001)

Santelmo, Vincent *The Official 30th Anniversary Salute to GI Joe 1964–1994* (Krause Publications, 1994)

Taylor, NG *Action Man: On Land, At Sea and in the Air* (New Cavendish, 2003)

Turpen, Carol *Baby Boomer Toys and Collectables* (Schiffer, 1998)

Various authors *Tomart's Encyclopedia of Action Figures* (Black Dog and Leventhal, 2000)

Walsh, Tim *Timeless Toys* (Andrews McMeel Publishing, 2004)

Ward, Arthur *Classic Kits* (Collins, 2004)

Author Bibliography

The Model World of Airfix (Bellew & Higton, 1983)

A Nation Alone (Osprey, 1990)

Resisting the Nazi Invader (Constable, 1997)

Airfix. Celebrating 50 Years of the Greatest Kits in the World (Harper Collins, 1999)

Classic Kits (Harper Collins, 2004)

Buying & Selling Wartime Collectables (Crowood, 2006)

Classic Toys (Crowood, 2006)

TV & Film Toys (Crowood, 2007)

Army Cap Badges (Crowood, 2007)

The Boys' Book of Airfix (Ebury, 2009)

Churchill's Secret Defence Army (Pen & Sword, 2012)

The Other Side of Airfix (Pen & Sword, 2012)

A Guide to Wartime Collectables (Pen & Sword, 2013)

Wartime Publications (Pen & Sword, 2015)

INDEX